DON'T PUT YOURSELF ON TOAST

DON'T PUT YOURSELF ON TOAST

FREDDY TAYLOR

Published in 2022 by Short Books
an imprint of Octopus Publishing Group Ltd
Carmelite House, 50 Victoria Embankment
London, EC4Y 0DZ
www.octopusbooks.co.uk
www.shortbooks.co.uk

An Hachette UK Company
www.hachette.co.uk

10 9 8 7 6 5 4 3 2 1

A CIP catalogue record for this book is available
from the British Library.

978-1-78072-527-7

The author and publishers gratefully acknowledge permission to
reprint copyright material in this book as follows:
Mary Schmich in the *Chicago Tribune* © Chicago Tribune 1997
All rights reserved. Distributed by Tribune Content Agency
"Going Up the Country" © Alan C Wilson and Canned Heat 1967

Jacket design © Gray318

Printed and bound in Great Britain by Clays Ltd, Elcograf S.p.A.

This FSC® label means that materials used for the
product have been responsibly sourced

MIX
Paper from
responsible sources
FSC® C104740

Prologue

What you are about to read comes from a journal I kept at the time of these events. It is interspersed with entries from my stepmother's medical diary. I wrote this for myself – but I also hope it might provide a little help to anyone else going through a similar experience.

Two shooks

Mary Schmich, a *Chicago Tribune* columnist, once wrote a column entitled "Advice, like youth, probably just wasted on the young". In 1998, Baz Luhrmann took her words and turned them into the number one single "Everybody's Free to Wear Sunscreen". There has always been one sentence that has spoken to me: "The real troubles in your life are apt to be things, that never crossed your worried mind, the kind that blindsides you at 4pm on some idle Tuesday." For me, it was at 8.45am on an idle Friday, aged 21.

White Wandsworth light creeps around the blinds in my bedroom and an audiobook is still playing from the night before. I arrange all my pillows into a mound of feathered comfort and feel full of an elementary sort of calm, the kind that arises after asking myself, "Is there anything nasty looming in the distance?" and the response is, "Nothing".

This is my last, never-ending summer before I return to university in Edinburgh in September. Four months of empty head, empty days; and a trip to the Greek island of Paxos with my dad, his girlfriend Bev and my 14-year-old sister Sophie. We are due to fly out on Monday.

My phone vibrates. "Pond Cottage" appears on the screen. My dad, Rod, isn't in the country; he flies back tonight, so it must be Bev. Her voice is clear and distinctive.

"Something's happened to Rod. He just called me from a taxi making no sense, repeating the same sentences and parroting words like 'suitcase'."

Dad has an unyielding work ethic and for the past ten years he's travelled extensively; on average he is away for 260 days of the year, but Bev knew this wasn't just some form of extreme jetlag, or exhaustion.

She tells me she had immediately called his travel agent and one of his colleagues to find out where he was and to try to ensure he didn't get on a plane.

I look down at my bare feet and notice a bruise on my left one. Bev continues.

"I waited till I heard before calling you. They managed to find him. He was in the British Airways lounge in Mumbai Airport. He had been aggressive towards lounge staff, vomited in the reception and passed out on one of their sofas. They thought he was drunk and were threatening to call the police."

Dad doesn't really drink but when he does the result is somewhere between a jovial master of ceremonies and Winnie-the-Pooh, after he's eaten all the honey.

I'm sitting on the floor. My legs crossed. Pins and needles prick my toes. My bent back is hot from the morning sun. I begin to pull repeatedly at the dry skin on the back of my heel. I haven't said anything.

Bev speaks with more urgency. "Your dad was lucid, panicked about missing his flight home but kept falling unconscious. They called an ambulance."

"Where is he now?" I ask.

"The critical care unit in Seven Hills Mumbai; he'll be there until his surgery. I'm about to leave to sort an emergency visa then I'll fly to Mumbai. This is the first moment I've had to call you. Their guess is a stroke, but we'll know more after the surgery. He's extremely agitated and very confused."

"What kind of surgery?"

Bev's strength begins to crack. "Brain."

I just sit there. I can't really gauge how I should react. Surgery in India. I'll admit the words conjure hacked limbs and infected bandages. Throw in "brain" and it's game over. Frantically, she announces her taxi has arrived.

"I'll call you as soon as I can."

She puts down the phone and I hold it against my ear, listening to the white noise until the phone hangs itself up. A cloud of dread has crept into my boyhood bedroom, bringing with it a steadily encroaching power that threatens to sweep away everything that once seemed indestructible. I try to stand but the pins and needles have turned my legs to stumps. I think of the last thing I said to him. Probably "bye". How depressingly empty and fitting.

I reach for my laptop and google "brain surgery India".

Phoned Freddy.
Phoned Sophie.

BA 21:50 BA0437 flight tonight.
Photo, passport, doctor's letter: for emergency visa.

Dr Ashmad (Critical Care Unit). Dr Lawsam (Neurosurgeon).

Rod taken to CCU because it's his brain.
He would have died if he'd have got on the plane.
Need to operate to relieve pressure.
There is always larger risk operating on the brain.
May have to learn to talk again/speech therapy.
They might have to operate whilst I am in the air.

Possibly aneurism.
George (UK Doctor) said he is in very good hands in
Mumbai, better than UK hospitals. Get to him as soon as
possible to grant permissions if needed.

Did the lamp arrive?

From as early as I can remember I've had a feeling, almost like a premonition, that I would be one of those people whose dad would die when they were young. A single small thought that never went away. A voice in the back of my head saying, "It's going to happen."

When you grow up with that feeling, it can't help but affect your behaviour. You think about it every day. You begin to create a "risk of death" hierarchy for different modes of transport he's taking; trains being the lowest, planes by far the highest. You always pick up the phone and never flake on a weekend. You put strangers' litter in bins as a trade to protect him. You save texts from him on every phone you've had. You set reminders to resave voicemails he's left. You take his photo. You worry, endlessly. You hug. You kiss. And you tell him you love him.

Mum used to read aloud *War Game* by Michael Foreman to me when I was little. It was a story about a group of friends who left Suffolk village greens for the horrors of trench warfare, no-man's-land and a Christmas Day football match. It terrified me. Convinced that Dad was on the brink

13

of being enlisted, I removed the illustrated jacket slip, hoping the plain green cover would camouflage it amongst the other books and Mum wouldn't be able to find it and scare me further. I still remember the relief I felt when I was told he was too old to go to war.

Aged twelve, to improve my chances of actually passing Common Entrance, I moved to a weekly boarding house that my school owned for foreign pupils. My dad had started travelling all the time, so the worry of enlistment was replaced by the worry of him flying. I developed rituals that I had to perform before he flew to keep him safe. I would send him three texts and then call him until he answered. If my panics ran into the night and I couldn't sleep, my boarding master would let me leave a voicemail while he was mid-flight, hoping my message would keep him airborne. Even now, when I know that Dad doesn't have to travel for a month, I feel calmer.

I think my panic derived from Dad's dedication to his work, which was making television. When he was "in work", he treated home like a pit stop between productions. He started out on *The Saturday Show* up in the north of England, before moving across the Channel to produce coverage of the Tour de France. In 1993, he worked on his first game show, *Supermarket Sweep* with Dale Winton. This was followed by Bruce Forsyth's *The Price is Right*, *Blind Date* and *Wheel of Fortune*. Around 2000, he joined Celador and became the executive producer of *Who Wants to Be a Millionaire*. Some highlights include: asking Major Charles Ingram, the game-show cheat, to strip down so he could frisk him for wires and acting as a consultant on Danny Boyle's *Slum Dog Millionaire*. In 2008, Sony bought the rights to *Who Wants to Be a Millionaire* and Dad became responsible for reproducing the format across 55 markets.

I'm certain his continual prolonged work absences strengthened my premonition that he was going to die young and leave us.

31 July 2011

Seven Hills Mumbai
Blood clot on brain caused stroke.

Rod vomiting, confused, fully conscious but speaking in questions. He's alert. If normal, clot will dissolve in 4-5 weeks, then he can travel. If we find abnormality, we might need to treat the cause to prevent re-bleed.

Could be many causes, burst vessel, thrombosis. Need MRI.

Blood pressure unlikely to be the cause. Clot alone enough to operate but swelling in skull and further pressure can damage brain. Clot has damaged vision and possibly speech.
Brain functions have worsened. Possibly a result of dehydration.

Op will help identify cause of clot.

Will now operate to relieve pressure on brain and remove clot. 98% up to them. 2% up to God.

Fatso!

I picture my 60-year-old, five-foot-eleven, slightly rotund father lying unconscious on an operating table in India.

He was born in Singapore and lived there with his two brothers and sister until, aged nine, he was sent to Sutton Valence, a boarding school in England. It was not uncommon for boys who boarded in the 60s to be exposed to inappropriate behaviour from male teachers. He was a victim of such behaviour. He's told me enough, although never in any detail, for me to assume it must have caused him some damage.

As I was growing up, he could be a strict and capricious father. His work, albeit well paid, was somewhat sporadic and I could sense the internal struggle it caused. He would slip into periods of darkness, spending weeks anchored to the sofa, devoting himself entirely to the TV. When I was ten, Mum and Dad got divorced. My sister and I were given designated weekends with each of them, and their relationship was reduced to doorstep shouting matches or muted, transactional exchanges. He was deeply unhappy. Take the pain of having to collect your children late on a Friday, from a house that meant so much, throw in a bad day at work and the result would be a monosyllabic father, only perking up around Sunday lunch. We could sometimes endure whole weekends of his silence, tiptoeing around him while he watched TV. We were never scared of him, however, and such weekends were the exception; we just knew that it was best not to poke the bear. His moods never extend into anger. The most violent thing I have witnessed him do was yell and kick at the frozen front wheel of his immobile car after he had left it in the Heathrow car park for ten icy days in January.

If those are his devils, his angels take the form of generosity and demonstrative kindness. He is always the first to open his wallet to pay for a round, even if his wallet is empty. He re-mortgaged his cottage twice to cover our school fees, but he never told Sophie or me and was the only dad to kiss his teenage son goodbye at the gates.

He is a gregarious, loud and competitive game-maker; someone capable of turning Sunday lunches with friends into hordes of children, chaotically screaming and avoiding being caught by "Rodney the British Bulldog". This spirit doesn't stop at children's games: he once gatecrashed a corporate city firm's black-tie Christmas party. Wearing all leather and carrying a video camera, he had adopted the pseudonym, Mike Ziminski, head of PR. The climax of the evening was always the waltz competition, which the Chairman and his wife won without fail, every year. Dad appointed himself judge, and to everyone's dismay, proceeded to ask the couple to leave the dance floor in the first round. The band stopped

Stroke on right side of brain.

Removed clot, found tumour, may be malignant. Took it out.

Sent tissue for exam. 3-4 days until report.

Rod under sedation.

Whose dog is that?

It's 8am in Paxos. I lie on my back, on a single bed under a cotton sheet looking at the ceiling fan whirl. It's close to 30°C. Cicadas and crickets vibrate the air. A wire mesh covers every window of the two-bedroom, white concrete bungalow. I scratch a new mosquito bite on my wrist and wonder what day he'll arrive.

My sister and I flew to the island three days ago by ourselves. By chance, Mum and her husband Peter are holidaying on the same island. Sophie is staying with them. She was four when Mum and Dad divorced and found it exceptionally hard to accept it or the arrival of new partners. Her foul moods were reminiscent of Dad's; and she used them to full effect on Peter and Bev. It was difficult. The idea of a shared holiday would have been out of the question. But now she's a happy teenager, for the most part, and too kind to subject anyone to the same levels of spite.

Under a towel my phone buzzes; it's Mum, asking if I'll meet them for breakfast at the harbour. I flip-flop my way down the boiling tarmacked hill towards the boats. The earth in the fields is dry and dark olives litter the sides of the road.

Little boats rock against the jetties. I weave through the res-
taurants' dusty laminated menu displays and the cushioned
bamboo armchairs that crowd the pavements.

I spy the three of them walking down from the other side
of the harbour. Mum seems to have a perma-tan wherever
she goes – put her under the sun for two hours and her skin
browns. She's a 51-year-old aerobics instructor and will probably still be able to pull off a bikini long into her eighties. She
has blonde highlights and a mouth Jagger would be jealous
of. With her unbounded optimism, she has the ability to get
enthusiastic about almost anything.

We order. I'm drinking iced orange juice with a paper
parasol. In Mumbai, Dad's having his drinks intravenously. I fidget in the bright heat, suddenly resenting being
here, remorseful at the prospect of a calamari lunch and dis-
cussions over which beach to sunbathe on.

"Stony or sandy?" Mum calls out, but her phone rings.
She looks at the screen and passes it straight to me. I stand
up and walk towards the boats to answer it.

"Hello boy."

I haven't heard his voice in six days, so at the sound of
it, I feel the blood rush to my chest. He sounds raspy and
his speech is slow. He's breathing heavily after each sentence
and the words take longer to come out, but it's him. Sophie
moves to stand beside me.

"How's the head?" I ask.

"Numb. I can't really see out of my left eye and my peripheral vision has gone from both."

Dad pauses.

"There are a few answers we need and checks to do before we can fly."

He takes a moment and breathes out. It stings to hear your dad cry. Especially when you are 5000 miles away. Suppressing the trembling in his voice, he asks to be passed on to Sophie.

"Speak tomorrow."

I watch her skip down the jetty towards me, before handing the phone over.

I turn towards Mum and answer, "Stony!"

Come on, get tougher

I use my towel to wipe condensation from my bathroom mirror. My face and chest are pink from falling asleep in the sun. My laptop is open on my bed and The Byrds are playing out of the speakers. I have an hour before dinner so I'm taking my time. I start combing my hair. Side parting. Straight back. Middle parting. The beak. The punk. I'm Kevin McCallister prancing.

Phone rings. It's Dad. He sounds worn out and serious.

"Are you busy?"

"No." A waft of hair gel goes up my nose.

"The doctors took some tissue samples from my brain during the operation. We got the results this evening."

He wastes no time, hardly breathing between sentences.

"I've got glioblastoma. It's an aggressive kind of cancer of the brain, Fred."

Sledgehammer. The word you hope you never have to deal with just crash-lands into your life. My Dad has cancer. A burning sensation in my chest shoots up and around my ears. I feel a sudden need to get dressed and grab a T-shirt. "We found out half an hour ago."

While he was being given that news, I was strutting about.

That innate feeling that has been with me all along has finally forced itself into fact. I try to blink but my eyes are too dry, and it stings. A hangnail catches as I run my fingers down the mosquito netting and I note a dozen dead insects on the windowsill.

Dad asks me not to tell Sophie and explains that he should be released to fly in three days. His voice lifts.

"I can't wait to see you."

I can't speak.

I phone my girlfriend, Emily. We share a flat in Edinburgh with three others and have been dating for seven months. She's from Cheshire, has long, dark-brown hair, beautiful, wide blue eyes and sounds a bit like a mouse. She says all the things you're supposed to say, then starts crying. She's a kind person. I'm phoning because I think it's what you're supposed to do. Talk to someone, seek comfort. But I feel this overwhelming sense of self-indulgence, as if I'm holding out a can and asking for people's tears. I'm wasting energy. Seeking sorrow when sorrow will do nothing to help.

We have dinner outside at a roadside restaurant with bright-blue plastic tablecloths, matching chairs and Coca Cola-branded parasols. Amongst a dozen tables, I look around and notice at least half have three generations seated around them. I watch parents who can only be ten years older than myself and I feel distinctly jealous that their parents have got to meet their children. The most important man in my life might not be around to answer my questions, meet the significant people I've yet to meet and spend time with his grandchildren. This realisation empties me of all hope, leaving me motionless in my seat. As I stare towards one family, a rage envelopes me. I grab one of the plastic table legs until my knuckles whiten. How can some be allowed to reach those milestones without relative tragedy while others are swallowed by it? The grandpa looks over and my anger is extinguished by a tremendous weight of sadness and sorrow, which I'm helpless to defeat. I revert to a childhood tactic and start to bargain with myself, striking imaginary deals to ensure my dad's safety, trying to find as many ways as I can to shift karma in his favour.

Mum knows something is up and, while Peter takes Sophie to choose some ice cream, I tell her. My beautiful mum, cheery as hell, moves to crouch down beside me, taking my hand and speaking softly.

"Your dad is the most dogged man I know. He's going to be fine."

The table next door is looking.

"What can we do to help?" she asks.

"I'd like to go home."

"OK, let me talk to Pete."

"Don't tell Sophie."

"No, OK."

You...

Sophie and I catch the first ferry of the morning across to mainland Corfu. There is no wind, and a low haze sits on the water. My eyes are red from the early start and the tears. She's confused as to why we are leaving and not waiting for Dad to arrive.

"He's flying home the day after next and I thought it would be better to meet him when he lands."

She goes very quiet. Like her dad, she can slip off into long periods of silence, unable to will herself out. But this is different. Her eyes don't look for answers in mine. We are both at the stern, standing. Six years' age difference is a lot when you're growing up. We're not friends. Arguments over nothing used to escalate into screaming matches. When things were at their worst, living apart, one of us with Mum, the other with Dad, was tabled as an option. That was five years ago and now we're both a little older. We've shaken off all that surface crap and we get on. I put my arm around her shoulders. We might not be friends but the bombs have started dropping and all I want to do is protect her.

Opposite us is a plump German couple in their sixties.

They have kind, sunburnt faces. I ask them if they wouldn't mind taking a photo of us. I don't think there will ever be a photo that better captures the love I have for my sister than that one.

Glioblastoma; the most aggressive type of cancer within the brain. Almost always fatal.

Tumour is in the Wernicke's area of the brain, temporal lobe. Damage to this area is likely, can result in meaningless speech, often with paraphasic errors and newly created words or expressions (dysphasia). A loss of vision likely too.

Return Wednesday to hospital to remove clips.
Lost a field of vision.
Haemorrhage caused brain damage.
Some damage reversible, can't tell at the moment.

Removed as much of tumour/cells as possible.
Need to see radiation oncologist and medical oncologist (chemo).
Possibility of cancer cells coming back is very high.
To prevent – needs radiation and chemo.

Start Levetiracetam – suppresses fits (brain scars can cause epilepsy). Highest risk 1st three months. Stop if no fits after that time.

Rod OK to fly Wednesday evening.

Surgical cap to protect wound.

Don't go through metal detector before Monday.

Visit ophthalmic dept to check field of vision.

Rad for 5 weeks.

Chemo can also start.

Will prob lose hair from rad. Will grow back. 3 months repeat.

MRI to check all clear.

Primary grade 4 but waiting for report to confirm. If so 50% chance of coming back in 2 years. 80% in 5 years. Option of operating again on tumour. Can survive 5-6 years with recurrence. 10-12 years without.

No cure, it's about buying time.

I want a bone and I want to be caught

Heathrow Terminal 5. The arrival gate has only a trickle of people coming through and I daydream about how nice it would be to rollerblade across the highly polished floor, from one end of the terminal to the other. Sophie is with me; she's not really a morning person and her face, like mine, looks different in the morning. We both sleep on our front, so gravity, over seven hours, tends to shift things around a bit.

Dad and Bev's flight arrives on time. A steady flow of passengers begins to come through the automatic doors. We wait as the stream thins to only one passenger every 20 seconds. Another scrum of people surges and out comes Dad, using the trolley, steadily walking towards the metal barrier wearing a charcoal suit, white shirt and blue tie. His black shoes are as shiny as the floor. The bandage wrapped around his head is the only thing that makes him stand out. Bev looks exhausted. We rush towards them. The two of us squeezing Dad and covering him with kisses. The unmistakable, faint smell of Dior Fahrenheit floats from him. This

32

scent is synonymous with Dad. If I ever catch a whiff of it in a supermarket, a waiting room, on the high street, or on a bus, I think of him.

Sony have organised a driver to take us home to Farnham. Before we've even left the terminal car park, Bev is asleep in the front. Dad sits in the back in between my sister and me. It's midweek and early so there is very little traffic. We don't speak. I'm used to our silent car journeys, when Dad is too deep into a mood to converse, but this is different. There is something in the boot that we are going to have to deal with when we get home, luggage we'll carry into the house and unpack, so until then, we'll face the road in front and hold hands.

Three years ago, Pond Cottage was quite different. Dad bought it after the divorce, when I was ten and Sophie was four. It was an 1800s, semi-detached, two-bedroom cottage with a 1960s time-capsule kitchen. After Bev moved in, the cottage was modernised and expanded. We walk up the long path through the garden and, as I look at the colourful flowers in bloom I'm reminded of Bev's wonderfully wild and knotted hair.

Carrying his bags inside, I walk past the oldest part of the cottage, the snug. When the house was renovated it was the only room to be left alone. It's small and carpeted. Two squashy red sofas with their backs against the wall fit into the corner, making an L-shape. Thick yellow fabric curtains are drawn back across the two windows, but aren't long enough to reach their bottoms. There's a large open fireplace with a wooden mantelpiece. Stacks of dry wood line either side of the grate. A large still life of a flowerpot painted by my great-grandfather hangs above it. And next to it there's an old, square television. The snug is the heart of the cottage and completely perfect.

I watch Bev help Dad upstairs and marvel at how well she deals with him and how normal she's being. They've been together for seven years. Aged 45, Bev is fourteen years younger than him. And at almost six foot, she's an inch taller than Dad and a lot slimmer. Her temperament is rational and calm; I've never heard her yell. She works within a communications sector for the government; she knows how to ask you things and she knows when to listen. Despite having girlfriends after Mum, Dad kept Sophie and I separate from them. Bev is the only one we've ever met and we're close.

Quietly, Bev beckons me to go and see him. The landing is steamy from his shower. Dad sits on the bed in his towel. His tummy always looks bigger sitting down. He's wearing a T-shirt that reads "Life is short so ski your ass off". I'm not sure if he chose it intentionally.

"I want to be as truthful as I can be about this."

I look at the floor then up to him.

"It's grade four brain cancer."

"What does that mean?"

"Grade one, you've caught it early, best chance of curing it. Grade two tumours don't grow fast but they can come back after treatment. Grade three spreads fast and is more likely to return after treatment. Grade four tumours are more aggressive. Treatment can extend life but not cure it."

"What's grade five?"

"Too late to do anything really."

I ask the question to avoid what he's just said.

His voice becomes optimistic. "Still, it might be two years, five years; could even be ten years."

For a moment I picture Dad in old age, wrapped up in the snug, watching test match cricket. But I know this isn't going to happen. Dad puts his hand on my knee to stop it bouncing.

"Your sister starts working towards her GCSEs next year, so I don't want you to tell her about the timeline. I want her to focus on them, not me. I'm going to tell her what I have and what we're going to do to treat it. I don't want her worrying when none of us know the extent of this."

I get up to leave the room. Dad clenches his fist and puts it on his chest.

"Sophs, come and see Dad," I call.

She comes bounding up the stairs, running past me happily, oblivious and young. I notice the freckles across her nose, her gorgeous smile, her gentle dark-brown eyes and her long, uncombed hair. I stand in my bedroom and open the window. I can hear Dad's deep voice. Then comes the crying.

Where are the little birds that fell off?

I've tried to write but don't really know what to write. My dad has brain cancer. I see the words, but I can't make sense of them. The statement feels like a private cry for attention on pages nobody will ever read. I need to just carry the knowledge and plead in quiet moments that he becomes the stat that defies the statistics. *Daily Mail* articles about modern medicine advancements and miracle recoveries flash through my head. I writhe and wonder how Dad's article ends.

I've called Bev several times this past month. She's sympathetic to the questions Sophie and I ask her. Her dad died two years ago. She never pretends to know all the answers and writes down anything I'd like her to ask Dad's doctors. A lifeguard watching over him, helping us feel more at ease. A mole to reveal how Dad's really coping, she tells me when he's up, when he's down and what brings it on. She'll let me know when he needs us to call and which nights are best to stay. I don't dare think about how much more frightening this would be if he was by himself.

An email arrived today from the head of Edinburgh's design course. It outlines what she expects of us in our final year and ends with "see you all in ten days". I resolve then that I'm not going to tell them; I don't want the sympathetic advantage. I want to know whatever I achieve this year will be without the aid of "special circumstances" bonus points and without anyone whispering knowingly.

Dr Gregory. Metal head staples removed. Treatment asap
buts need recovery time. Mon-Fri radiotherapy, 10 mins, quick
in and out. Follow-ups are once a month. Very rare that this
cancer will spread to other parts of the body or new parts of
brain. Operation in India – even best surgeon leaves some
cells behind and needs treatment.

Radiotherapy side effects will be short-term and go away –
very rarely can cause brain problems. Can develop seizures
long-term. Stroke risk high. May lose some hearing in right ear.
Keep him busy. Don't spend time sitting and thinking.

Chemo – can be mornings and evening. Needs empty stomach (incl. water) an hour before and after taking. Needs to
consider social life. Advise anti-sickness pills at same time for
first few days. Vision – won't get worse than it is. But on basis
of eye report unlikely to drive again.

GBM – short name for tumour.
Help available – life coach for kids as well if needed.

Further than the sea goes

I love taking the train from Kings Cross to Edinburgh, partly because of the open expanse of sea, just before Berwick-upon-Tweed and partly because it stretches the elastic that bit further from who I am in London, making me feel bigger than "Fred from Wandsworth". It's getting dark as I walk up the sloping taxi entrance out of Waverley and away from the glowing Princes Street hub. I'm too late for the bagpipe buskers, but the familiar smell of hops wafts up my nose as I brace myself for the News Steps. There are easier ways to ascend into Old Town but I climb them because, from the top, the view of the city's orange street lamps, Calton Hill's follies and the ancient soot-stained buildings remind me of my grandparents, lazy, sunny days basking in Princes Street Gardens and my independence.

I'm the last housemate to arrive back for the start of our final year. In the first term of the first year, I met Anna. She's the best friend I've made here. I enjoy her company more than anyone's. She studies animation and is dedicated. Liam's a quiet lad from Bradford, tall and skinny. His manners make him feel like someone from a nineteenth-century novel. He owns one pair of trousers, three shirts and three V-neck jumpers. He smokes like a chimney and studies painting. We all think he's going to be the next Hockney. I've known Daisy since I was fifteen, we can irritate the hell out of each other but I'm very fond of her. She studies costume design with Emily and has a small addiction to eBay. There are always a million reference tabs open on her laptop. They all know about Dad.

We rent a Victorian tenement flat, 17C, Lutton Place, just off South Clerk Street; a two-minute walk from Pollock Halls and the Commonwealth swimming pool. From the top windows you can spy the peak of Edinburgh's mountain, Arthur's Seat. Chipped front-door paint reveals brighter colours beneath the black gloss. My bedroom walls are covered in screenprint posters, nicely designed flyers and a mood board of home. My grandfather's Heriot-Watt university scarf is held up with masking tape above an open fireplace that I'm definitely not allowed to use, but do. The window looks out onto the street. Opposite is a large church called St Peter's. Apart from the obligatory service at Christmas, churches and religion don't really hold much significance in my life. In fact, I've never really acknowledged it. But now being back north, so far away from Dad, St Peter's stands tall and welcoming.

"Dinner."

Anna has cooked a veggie lasagne, Daisy's made a bean salad, Liam's doing something with a big tomato, Emily's on tea duty and for a whole evening I don't think about Dad.

You have to hit me with the toaster, whenever you like

The Sunday morning bells wake me up reminding me to go to the church that evening. After an arduous day in the library, struggling to balance my course projects with my dissertation, I cycle home in the dark. I lock my bike on the railings, cross the road and duck in through the large doors of St Peter's, checking first that there isn't a service going on. I never go in when there is.

Inside, huge iron pipes run along the sides of the walls, radiating heat. It smells like a proper church, that mix of dust, old carpet, wooden chests and lingering frankincense. The nave is about 50 metres long and the hammerbeam roof is a stained dark timber supported by ten columns of polished, pinkish-grey granite. The windows are stained glass but I've never seen them with the light passing through. Ruby-red paint, with a gold fleur-de-lis pattern, covers the walls. Dark oak pews sit either side of the aisle, matching the ceiling. The door to the priest's quarters stays open. Whenever I visit, I sit in the back right-hand corner of the church, where it's dark and I can't be seen. I'm here to negotiate with someone I don't believe in; I'm here to will Dad's condition into improvement.

Tonight, I slip inside to find the church occupied by about seven or eight people scattered amongst the pews. I stand in the doorway on the brink of turning away but pause for a moment. The priest is talking about sickness. I listen as he speaks of it as a burden. He compares it to a stone. In his hand is a smooth pebble. He holds it above a baptismal font filled with water and invites people up.

"Take this pebble in your hand and think of the person for whom you are here, then drop it into the water."

One by one the smattering of people take their turn, closing their eyes as they drop the pebble into the basin. I join the back of the queue. Light this candle, eat this biscuit, drink this wine. I would have dunked my entire head in that basin if he'd told me to. I close my eyes and drop the pebble. It might be the ceremony of it, or perhaps the nine pairs of eyes on me, but despite my scepticism the moment feels significant. My neck tingles like when someone strokes the hair on your head. I open my eyes to see the pebble touch the bottom of the basin with a dull clink. The priest smiles and I turn away, surprised I partook and certain that was enough openness for today. I walk out into the cold Edinburgh night and into the Mosque Kitchen for an Indian takeaway.

Nothing definite to be seen that's of concern on the scan.
That's good news. There's a hole in the brain and some areas
which may be post-surgical residual disease, can't tell more
currently. Looks favourable. Good starting point. Need time to
tell. 3-6 months until next review.

Chemo to start next week. Seven days a week for 6 weeks.
Then break for 4-5 weeks. Then second phase of chemo
begins. Unlikely to cause sickness but will get anti-sickness
medication in case.

Second weeks of chemo will be most tiring /more side-
effects.
No restrictions – give him what he wants.

Last day of radio. Rod is doing very well but can't guarantee anything. Tiredness could kick back in stronger 3-4 weeks after.

Chemo new dose Nov 16th. Sickness and vomiting likely.

MRI week before. Do not get excited at this stage. Little cells will be in the process of death – causing cells to swell, therefore creating pseudo progression.

Baby shampoo and E45. Hair loss over course – towards the mid/end.

Rod mentioned feeling exhausted but still maintaining exercising and swimming.
Keep drinking fluids.
Reading will improve after 3 months.
Speech and language therapist will get in touch.

Next MRI booked for 20th January will be better indication of state of tumour.

Mexican sexiford

I'm 22 today. My flatmates poke their heads around the door and wake me with bed pouncing, kisses and handshakes. A few of my course pals take me for £1.50 bacon-and-egg birthday baps just up from the Grassmarket but decline to come over later to celebrate. It's only when I'm walking up my street and spy familiar silhouettes through our living-room window that I realise Emily has organised a surprise party.

I'm greeted with loud jeers, an impressive but rather unflattering cake of my face made by Emily, beautifully crafted homemade cards and a Victorian paraffin heater, a treasure bought by all of my flatmates down at Leith's Sunday car boot sale.

After everyone has left, I climb into bed and open a card from Dad. His writing is messier than normal and illegible in places. Like Mum, he never writes more than the usual birthday pleasantries and this year is no exception. Regardless, this card could be the last one I ever get, so I'll be holding onto it.

Do you want to see my ride?

Sophs called me this morning in quite a state. In a preemptive move to make friends and family more comfortable with the inevitable "chemo-balding", he bought a hair trimmer from the local Boots and proceeded to buzz his entire head, grade zero. He was so pleased with himself he sent a selfie to practically everyone in his phonebook. Rodney, a presentable, shirt-wearing, soft-around-the-edges man, now resembled a hardened, senior(ish) citizen, who looked very pleased to be leaving Wandsworth Prison.

Visual field test. Right eye slightly better. Left eye slightly worse. Averaging about the same. Left and right mid-far peripheral vision is a problem. V weak. Speech and reading not improving. Recommended Rod should be reassessed for his reading problem. Has been in contact with a speech specialist who will be in touch. They could recommend someone local to home.

Appointment with Sira (speech and language therapist) at the Marsden.

Speech disorder: dysphasia, a condition that affects your ability to produce and understand spoken language. Can also cause reading, writing, and gesturing impairments.

Have you seen my leathers?

Bad day today. I've been thinking about my time and where I should really be spending it. Dad's been on chemo for a month, sitting in some municipal chair while his body is intravenously drip-fed poison. I get sad whenever I think he might be lonely or sitting by himself.

I'm a four-minute walk from Emily and her costume department but I go straight home from the studio. She'll have her head down and I don't really feel like pretending to her I've had a good day. Inside Anna and Daisy are stretched out across the living-room sofas, about to start a film. I slip away to the church. The heating is off and the huge iron pipes are cold. I'm grateful for my extra layers. I think about how different it will feel next month, with Christmas around the corner and all the decorations that come with it. I stay for an hour before crossing the road and returning home.

I've been caught out. Anna and Daisy spy me in the hall-way and ask where I've been. As I speak, I'm overcome and begin to cry. I don't know why it hits me so hard. I collapse into a heap and confess, embarrassed and desperate. I explain that I am trying anything I can to fix my dad. They huddle around, sheltering me like a den.

Chug, chug, chug

I submitted my dissertation draft, title and plan last week. "The Use of Photographs as a Way to Visualise and Communicate Statistical Information." They've predicted me a D grade. Mostly because I kept tripping the reader up with "nonsensical gobbledegook".

Dad calls most days. He cares a lot about my work, even if he doesn't fully understand it. He is logistics and numbers and I film flaming pillows floating on lochs. Dad does not deal well with his children's failings. He could easily avoid speaking to me for a fortnight if I didn't live up to his academic expectations. He would express his disappointment with a silent fury. I do all I can to avert such situations. As this D is only a prediction, I think it's best kept to myself, given the circumstances.

Dr Patrick – Blood tests fine, if anything improved.
Up to full dose of chemo (420) for next 4 months.

Rod can start thinking about going back to work.
Talk in the new year about plans/issues about reintegration.

We should feel positive.

Pass me the river

Train to London tomorrow. It's raining hard outside and there's a river running down our street. The girls have all gone home for the holidays, so the flat is quiet, just how Liam likes it. I crank up the heating and walk into his room with a tea, pack of Tunnock's and my laptop. The ceilings are tall and the single-pane window is rattling in its frame. He's smoking, listening to Radio 4 and carefully working on a postage-stamp-size painting. We don't normally have much to say to each other, but he probably senses I could do with the company. We sit, working in relative silence for five hours. He's smoked eight roll-ups, drunk four cups of tea and declined any tomato soup. It's one of those evenings that's completely unremarkable but serves as a restorative pit stop before heading south and facing Dad's illness.

6 month MRI scan results with Dr Patrick Gronam.

Recommends more surgery.

Likely damage will be caused.

Scan pretty good but GBM still there. Unlikely to be radio necrosis (dead cells), more likely persistent tumour. Relatively simple to remove – the more we take the better. But the more we take the greater the risk to speech etc.

Operation – craniotomy. Local anaesthetic but awake.

Vision on right almost bound to get worse.

If speech worsens during the op they'll stop. Verbal stuff can be worse at first but improve post op.

Start the op with Rod asleep. Open up head. Wake Rod up and talk to identify areas to preserve, then focus on remaining tumour. Then send back to sleep and close up. If tumour is in middle of speech area there will be very little they can do surgically. No point having the worst of both worlds though. Speech and vision affected and still have tumour.

Median is 50 out of 100 dead in a year. He is young, fit and positive. It will improve things and keep quality. Can operate again after if we need to but restrictions come when operating on such an important part of the brain. Be positive it does improve things and prolongs quality for 15 months – 2 years.

Bluebells all around her

It's Christmas Eve. We were meant to be in Costa Rica with Mum, Peter and his two grown-up kids this Christmas. For obvious reasons plans changed. Shortheath Road is silent and all I can hear is the trickle of next door's garden fountain.

I hear Dad shuffle up the stairs. He puts his head around my door.

"Big day tomorrow. Sleep well, my boy."

He then treads along the corridor into Sophie's room. Muffled through the wall, I hear him singing softly to her. The same song he's sung to her before bed, all her life:

You are my sunshine, my only sunshine.
You make me happy when skies are grey.
You'll never know, dear, how much I love you,
So please don't take my sunshine away.

They're both crying as they sing the last line together. I think about how many more times he'll get to sing it to her; I roll over and begin to sob into my pillow.

The chain won't slip off

Edinburgh in January is quite the contrast to Edinburgh in December. The German Christmas market has been packed away, the ice rink has left its soggy mark on the grass of Princes Street Gardens, grey slush litters the street and the fairy lights from Hogmanay hang forlornly tangled above.

It's Tuesday, around 7pm. I walk through our building's front door to our tenement flat. There's a new scribble on the wall in some sort of Glaswegian dialect and the row of locked bikes at the bottom of the stairs has now become a pile. The flat is empty. With deadlines looming and four months until final hand-in, most of our time is spent in our studios or in the library on George Square. I take a large glug of milk from the carton, sit at the table for a moment and then decide to call Pond Cottage.

Dad answers the phone. He always sounds so pleased to hear my voice. I don't tell him, but I've put him on loud-speaker and I'm recording the call on my laptop. This is the transcription:

"Hello, boy!"

"Hi, Dad."

"How you doing? All good? And Emily?"

"All OK, just booking a train to come and stay with you. I'll come straight to Farnham Station."

"Ah, that would be great. Just let us know what time and we'll be there."

"Where are you at the moment, Dad?"

"I'm on the loo [we both start to laugh]. Bit of a lazy start here. I haven't really been sleeping well."

He pauses for a moment.

"I need to just crack on, get stuff sorted so we can have the best time before next week."

His voice begins to shake.

"We met with the surgeon today and he made me feel very confident, very safe about what was going to happen on the operation table. I think the interesting thing is that I'm going to be able to talk to him whilst they do it. And he said if there is a reduction in quality it will be minimal."

"Reduction in quality." The phrase sticks with me. It means a loss or worsening of an entire human function. My mind spirals. Dad's about to have open-brain surgery for the second time. Like some sort of Russian roulette, I wonder which function will be affected. Memory? Sight? Will his entire personality shift? He sounds more worried than I've heard him before. The severity of the next week sinks in. Then he hardens.

"You've got to understand we're not dealing with a walnut here; we can't just chop it out. Imagine trying to remove a drop of black ink from a glass of water. That's what we're dealing with. The more water you take the less ink remains, but there's a limit to how much you can take. Try and understand, it's impossible to remove all of it."

I'm trying to reply but I muddle my words as the visualisation forms and hope fades.

"Ask any question you want." He softens. "I can be on the phone all day with you."

Returning to minor details, we talk logistics again, before a silence falls. Now it's Dad's turn to lose his words.

What follows is probably both the saddest and most open exchange with Dad I have ever had. I am so grateful to have it on record.

Shaking off the brutality of it all, he says, "I'm going to be here for you, but we've been told the treatments can only do so much."

He then speaks with an acute clarity.

"We've always known there's a limit to human life; it just seems that this limit is coming a lot sooner than I hoped."

He pivots cheerily. "Have you booked the Sheep Heid for graduation?"

"Yes, it's all booked."

"And the skittle alley?"

"Yes."

"We'll bowl on the same team, if you don't mind."

Just before we end the call, he thanks me for ringing. His voice sounds tired.

We hang up and I sit there. My cheeks are taut from tears. Flatmates clatter through the front door and I wipe my face. Nobody needs to come home to a crying flatmate and I don't feel like sharing what I'm feeling.

Ice, ice, ice

Pre-drinks in the flat. Daisy's doomed the evening by putting on Black Eyed Peas' "I gotta feeling". Whenever we've played it previously, someone would have a terrible night.

We walk down Newington Street, onto South Bridge and into a raucous house party. I'm greeted by familiar faces, eccentric sculptors, folk musicians and some trendies standing around an iPhone choosing music. There's not really enough room to dance but it's comforting to have a beer in hand and chat mundanely.

I hear shouting from the stairwell. The host is standing at the top of the stairs, kindly telling four leather-jacket-wearing chancers they're not welcome. It's a stand-off.

"I don't know yoos lot."

The banisters are now full of guests barking down.

They get it, they're not welcome and begin to leave. As they do, one of them calls the police and reports the house party. I rather stupidly follow them down and confront the snitch. That's when I get punched square in the face. First time ever. I stay on my feet and sway a little; it doesn't hurt but I can taste metal and feel my heartbeat in my lips. He's smiling wide, his janky teeth on show.

"Doesn't matter how hard you hit me, I'll never have teeth as bad as yours," I snap.

He hits me again, straight in the mouth. This one hurts, and splits my lip.

Guests intervene and chase them away down the main road. I'm taken upstairs past several, wide-eyed faces. I rather like the attention. A girl gasps. In the bathroom I can see why. I look like a botched Botox patient with teeth, cheeks and nose splattered in blood. It looks more dramatic than it is, but my whole face is throbbing and I've got a weird sensation in my temple.

I'd like some tennis

Temperatures dropped last night so cycling was somewhat hazardous this morning. My studio is on the fourth floor of Evolution House. I'm sitting in the glass corner facing north, towards Edinburgh's castle. Dad called. I didn't mean to start hysterically sobbing but how else was I supposed to react when he throws "I'll always be with you" at me? What makes matters worse is that all my course-mates will have heard me. I haven't told any of them, so they probably think I'm crying about my projects. That's embarrassing.

I take a walk towards the Meadows and call Mum. She always picks up, always sounds delighted and always cheers me up. First, she covers all the juicy gossip in her life. Then, she gives me a list of different distractions to try.

"Go shopping. Go running. Go to the pub. Take Emily out. Take Anna out. Take all your flatmates out – here I'll send you some money. Make a Guinness cake – here I'll send you the recipe. Go to the sea. Go go-karting. Get on a train to Wandsworth, you'd be here by supper and Peter could cook you that prawn curry you love."

She continues, more softly, "Figure out what tiny thing might help, and do it."

"Thanks, Mum."

I hang up and head to the animation department, where Anna and I make stupid videos on Photo Booth for most of the afternoon.

Craniotomy tomorrow.
Rod not sleeping.

Dr Gregory. Operation went well generally. Tested the tissue removed, not conclusive but not malignant. Need more tests though. Temp down to 38 now. Was feverish. Head pain. Very lethargic today + yesterday.

2-4pm visiting. Resume chemo once recovered. If chemo doesn't work, we can try an alternative.

Well behaved everybody, except Rodney

My lips have almost healed. I'm on the train to London, to visit Dad in St George's Hospital. By 7.30pm, I am sitting on the Northern line heading to Tooting. Half the carriage is standing. Sitting opposite me is a man wearing a Fat Face fleece. I think about Dad's questionable Fat Face collection. I get off the tube and walk towards the exit. It feels warm down here, until a strong February gust shoots along the exit stairs and stalks me all the way to St George's.

I walk through the doors and I'm greeted by the familiar pong of bleach that I imagine is stockpiled in every hospital's cleaning closet. Third floor, intensive care. I tentatively walk through the doors towards the unattended reception. I am here outside visiting hours, but they said I could come any time before nine.

Seeing my dad in hospital for the first time freezes me. His eyes are closed and tubes seem to be inserted into him everywhere. He looks more vulnerable than I have ever seen him.

His bed is at 45 degrees and all but one of the other cubicles have their curtains closed. With a sheet tucked around him, his arms stuck out by his side, and his head covered in so many bandages, he's Mr Bump. I wait for a nurse and then walk over to him. Up close, he looks even more frail. Wilted skin covers his hands and his stubble is greyer than normal. He's asleep.

I touch his arm gently and he wakes up. His eyes roll forward – taking about eight seconds before they adjust and recognise me. Immediately, he snaps an incoherent sentence at me.

"Turn it to clean, please."

I'm thrown. I look at his IV, his clean sheets, his bandages. All pristine.

He repeats the same sentence. Does he need the loo? Whatever it is, he's angry I'm there.

He changes his tack, confused that his idiot son clearly doesn't speak his language. "Bring the pipes down."

I explain that the nurses know I'm here, but he's becoming more and more agitated, speaking in forceful nonsensical whispers. I try to make conversation with him but he's insistent I go. I lift his hospital quilt over his tummy and kiss his hand goodnight. His hand is cold and his eyes are already shut.

Outside, I walk through Victorian terrace streets. I blame his muddled demands on the anaesthetic, but I know tissue vital to his language and speech has been removed and with it, seemingly, his ability to hear what he's saying and align words with their meaning. I am now starting to realise the damage his illness – and the treatment for it – is capable of and plead that his linguistic errors are temporary.

I want you to wash it and posh it and bring me back a hot one

Dad is recovering at Pond Cottage. For the last fifteen days Bev has been his day nurse and his night nurse but this week, a little worried about her job, she's started going back to work, Wednesdays and Thursdays. Although Dad has a rota of friends to step in, she hates leaving him. She hates the idea of him being alone all day.

This morning she called me with some nice news. She left for work, cycling down Shortheath Road to Farnham Station. When she went to lock up her bike, she realised she had forgotten her keys. She cycled back up the 20-minute hill home. On arriving, she grabbed her keys and headed upstairs to check on him. She could hear the shower running and as she got closer, shouting. She started to run along the landing until she realised Dad wasn't shouting, he was singing in the shower, belting out Don McLean's "American Pie" as loud as he could. She didn't disturb him and left him to it.

Crungie

It feels like spring outside. I run through the Meadows, spying bits of green pushing their way up the sides of the concrete tennis courts. In Marchmont, window boxes are coming to life and Sainsbury's has started selling daffodils.

I catch glimpses of my reflection in parked cars and acknowledge that I'm not a particularly graceful runner. Home and showered, I count eight small pock-mark scars on my cheeks in my bedroom mirror. I've been standing in front of mirrors and stretching them out of my face for three years. Fresh, angry red spots loom on my forehead and surround my mouth. Eight weeks ago, I started taking Roaccutane, the strongest treatment for acne, for the second time. It's blistered my lips so they're always bleeding and my skin hurts in direct sunlight, like a vampire. I've timed taking it so I don't have to borrow Emily's concealer for graduation. Fingers crossed.

30 March 2012

Dr Gregory. Post op. Reviewing ongoing treatment – tissue responding.

1st patient in 15 years to see healthy cells behave like normal tissue during treatment. Astonishing to see. Existing problems related to treatment have been taken care of by surgery. Want another 6 cycles of treatment to start (once approved) in 2 weeks. Then another scan in 3 months (Sept).

Now have proof that treatment (thought not to be working) is working.

We're in remission – not curing it. Means the signs of it are reduced.

Clear and naked

I've returned to Pond Cottage to break the back of my dissertation. It's a welcome change from the routine of Edinburgh, especially with Dad in remission. Bev is taking advantage of me being there and commuting every day. I'm working on the dining-room table, paper everywhere, and Dad's sitting outside in his hammock listening to Labi Siffre.

By the evening, I feel ready to hand him the first four pages. It doesn't go well. First, he struggles to actually read the words, and when I read it to him, he stops me after the third paragraph. Without stumbling or errors, he remarks, "How can I be expected to critique something when you're not helping me understand even the basics of what you're referring to. This isn't a PhD, you have to make your writing..." He pauses for a long time as he tries to find his words, "...comprehensible. You're better than this. Right?"

"Yep."

Bev arrives home and in a much gentler tone, corroborates Dad's advice. I feel like this is going to be a long week.

Rod returning to Sony, three days a week.
Next scan is after the summer, 4th September.

Kiss my rolls

Emily is very talented. She produces delicate samples which show off her skilful sewing techniques. Her work is backed up by thorough research of materials. She has deservedly breezed through each year, but this morning I heard her crying to Daisy in her room, distraught about her final project. Idly, I wonder if it's my fault as her boyfriend's family crisis means her head is filled with selfless ways to help, instead of allowing her to think of her own work. Or maybe she's just buckling under the pressure of finals.

I notice that I feel no urge to console her. If I was a better boyfriend, I'd be more empathetic but I don't respect her weakness. I know that's unkind, but when it comes to life concerns, I'm approaching the top of the mountain, with the wind howling about me, and she's sitting at base camp, toasty in her sleeping bag. Anyway, whatever she's dealing with, I'm glad she's got Daisy.

I think it's time to go

My wheel almost lodges itself in Edinburgh's unfinished tram tracks. I'm cycling across from Murrayfield up to Lauriston Place, towards the art college. On the front of my bike is a small plastic cage. Inside is "Snowflake", a white rabbit, and precious companion of a pal of mine. Snowflake is the star of a music video promo I'm shooting for next week's final major project hand-in.

The painting studios have been cleared out so there's ample space for shooting. The plan is to reveal multiple objects from under a flourish of golden fabric, leading up to the grand finale of Snowflake sitting on a spinning decorative Roman plinth. Simple.

Not so simple. Snowflake is now on the loose. The next three hours are spent building a maze to trap him and waving a carrot in the air. I spare a thought for the academic students of Edinburgh swotting in the library for their finals and wonder what they would make of my last days as a student. Despite Snowflake's best efforts, I get the shot. It's not perfect but the light is fading and I've had enough of this rabbit.

Laaaarge drink

The days following final hand-in are a blur of cocktails, trips to Cramond Island, *The Walking Dead* and onion bhajis. I'm hungover. Yesterday, Emily found me passed out in a cubicle at Wagamamas at 3pm, taxied me home and put me to bed with a bucket for company.

It's 6am. My eyes wince as I open my laptop. I've got an email from the head of Administration, titled "Dissertation". Gulp.

"We are delighted to inform you, your dissertation has been awarded the Katherine Michaelson Prize for outstanding thinking. Your work will be published by the University of Edinburgh Library and the prize money of £1400 will be awarded."

I'm dumbfounded. I'm whooping. I'm out of my overdraft. I'm about to be sick.

A big bouncy and a big jumpy, jumpy, jumpy

Sporting a rented black gown, I walk out of McEwan Hall into Bristo Square. The other clusters of families make me grateful that all mine are in attendance: Mum, Peter, Dad, Sophie, Bev and my grandma. Sophie runs up and high-fives me before I lift my 87-year-old grandma off the ground, spinning her as she squeals. It's the first time any of my friends have seen Dad since it all started, and his shining bald head looks a little menacing with the fresh, 10cm semi-circular scar on the side. People are staring but I don't care. We pose for the obligatory graduation photos and Dad gives me a copy of the *Herald* newspaper, as a keepsake. We're both wearing our Taylor Ancient tartan kilts, a mix of green, pink and purple hues that's only worn on occasions like these, and I am proud to be matching him.

The Sheep Heid, with its low ceilings and dark timber beams, boasts that it is Scotland's oldest pub. Brass trinkets decorate the walls surrounding our table. All my flatmates are here. I sit next to Mum, while Emily and Anna flank Dad. I marvel at how patient they're both being with him, never trying to finish his sentences or give him the words. More photos, more pints, and I feel grateful for the shaky normality we've managed to achieve.

Dad's been gone from the table for some time and Bev has begun to worry. I check the loo, bar and beer garden before peering inside the thirteenth-century skittle alley. Two parallel lanes run the length of the building, with dark marks scarring the polished ancient wood. Cannonball-sized balls line up along the middle and there, feverishly practising his bowling action, is Dad. The entire party are summoned and I out the competitive rogue. The game quickly descends into chaos, shoes flying, bodies on the lane, Guinness everywhere and very few skittles knocked over. Dad declares himself victor and only Anna contests it.

Two months ago, it felt as if we were preparing for the worst ride imaginable. Today, while we skirt carefully around the subject of life expectancy, it seems the combination of surgical and chemo treatments has worked. I pretend to be ignorant of the facts and embrace how good the day is. The ink has been halted. A disaster is to come but for now, it is held in abeyance. I want to believe that he will be the exception and defy statistics, but probability tells me that sometime in the next five years, the dam will burst and I'll lose my dad.

She's on the loo, it's all blue, what can we do?

Sophie, wearing a baby-blue dress, is mowing a huge 'R+B' loveheart into the grass at Pond Cottage. The kilts are on again and the sun is out. Dad and Bev are getting married today in a barn in Bentley. Bev's wearing a floral green trouser suit and carrying a modest bouquet of bright-purple thistles. Financially and legally, I think their marriage makes things simpler, but those do not feel like today's motives. Over this year, I have watched Bev change from his girlfriend into his temple of strength, his nurse, his motivator. She's been by his side in the trenches since the start and today is about recognising that.

The entire congregation rise to their feet and cheer, as the vows "in sickness and in health" are spoken. Then, despite having a golf-ball-sized piece of tissue removed from his brain, Dad takes to the pulpit to read his eight-page speech in size 20 font. What should take 20 minutes to read pushes past 50. Each utterance a fence to jump. Words no longer resemble themselves. Methodically tracing each sentence to ensure its completion. When he does go off script it becomes impossible to translate, but he acknowledges his weakness, jovially reprimanding anyone who attempts to put him off. When he loses his footing, pausing for longer than he should, friends rally from the back. And when he gets emotional, everyone gets emotional. His blazing speech ends with a verse from a poem his mum used to sing him:

> Here's to it and through it,
> for them that can do it,
> without any fumble at all.
> Up with it,
> down with it,
> God speed you well with it
> and jolly good luck to us all.

By 1am my cousin has commandeered the microphone and is slaughtering "Gangsta's Paradise". Emily is still going strong, I've mastered the art of twirling in a kilt while keeping my modesty, and for the first time since India, Dad's moving, shaking and dancing, with two large sweat patches across his chest to show for it.

An hour later, I'm bundling my drunk father and new stepmother into the back of a car. Just before I join them, Dad's friend George, an oncologist, takes me aside and mentions just how remarkable his recovery has been. "I think he's going to make it, you know."

I believe him.

They are having almost as much fun as I'm having against you

We're at Oak Park Golf Club for the biennial T-Cup, a family golf day. This also marks the first occasion he has been allowed behind the wheel since it all began. Naturally, when you've had your peripheral vision surgically sliced out of you, golf buggies don't go in straight lines. Despite having an entire fairway, we spend the afternoon frantically rushing and shouting instructions to ensure the electric motor only skims the rim of sandy bunkers. Frustrated and a little confused, Dad begins to see the funny side and even starts to drive into the back of other buggies intentionally, singing, "Sorry, I've just had a cran-io-tomy."

Hitting the white balls, however, was deemed not to be; after four and a half wild swipes and a lot of swearing, he gives up and retreats behind the wheel, from where he critiques my stance, swing, posture, club choice, grip, height of tee, foot, head and shoulder position.

I want to go dancing tonight

The cicadas are really going for it this evening. It's our last night in Paxos. Sophie and I hijacked the end of Dad and Bev's honeymoon. We've been staying on the other side of the island from where we were last July, but the sensation of taking that same ferry is sobering. Being back here makes me continually give a quiet thanks. It feels as if someone heard my fears and granted me this time.

Despite it not being the kind of place that requires reservations, we reserve a table for four, at that same restaurant with the blue chairs and Coca Cola parasols. Sophie and Bev are trying to figure out why Yeni raki goes cloudy with ice. They're closer than they've ever been. Whatever angst Sophie once used to hold against her has been rubbed away this year. I sit opposite Dad. His hazelnut-brown eyes meet mine and he smiles. I see the serenity in his face; he looks relaxed. We each order fish and show off our feeble tan marks. All the noise around us feels muffled, as if our table is wrapped in a cocoon of cotton wool.

I want this dinner to last as long as possible. There have been times this year where I've felt like a shallow tray of water: even the slightest knock would slosh out tears. But tonight feels significant, like a landmark. The tray feels steady.

Dad's tired. We order the bill and clamber into a taxi. I wind down the window and keep my eyes on our table as it's cleared. We turn a corner and roll into the dark, the table disappearing from sight.

MRI results for tumour.

Scan is unhelpful. Want to review further as affected area seems larger than area pre-op.

Biopsy – not ideal given how badly Rod recovered last time.

Larger area not advisable to operate as would cause damage. Last time was small in comparison.

Radio necrosis (dead tissue from radiotherapy) can be cause of appearance of affected area.

Feels like we're being prepped for bad news.

No more blue boys

Last week, I went for an interview at KesselsKramer, a thirteen-person design and advertising studio, based in Hoxton Square, London. This morning, I've received an email offering me an internship. I gladly accept. Only £25 per day, but still good news.

What are surgical options?
Scan shows quite a dramatic difference in growth
between last time and now. Not sure what we're looking at
though – could be tumour or could be just dead cells.
Dr Patrick keen to do biopsy today.

Biopsy results inconclusive.
Area looks like classic glioblastoma.
Is worse than last time round.

PET scan says it's abnormal and any invasive surgery recovery time would be very slow and could cause further issues and infections.

Despite this, think Rod would benefit from more surgery. Reopen existing entry point. Speech and vision will be more affected.

It could be RN/dead cells though, he's 50/50 – even with 15 years' experience – thinks it's safer to op just in case. Operation arranged for next week.

I'll have the chicken to start with lots of vonus

The circular front of the Royal Surrey County Hospital reminds me of the gas holders next to the Oval cricket ground. Different hospital, same pong. Flanking the doors are royal-blue, anti-bacterial hand gel dispensers; both read "alcohol free". I picture homeless people wandering in, wrapping their lips around the nozzles and drinking the stuff like a slush puppy. My hands are now hygienically sticky.

I take the mirrored lift up to the post-op ward. I am wearing one of Dad's oversized sweatshirts and I need a haircut. Upstairs the ward is silent. There's the low hum of a radio playing somewhere near a nurses' station. I'm told to wait.

Dad's been heavily sedated since yesterday's operation and is only really coming around now. A rotund and lovely nurse glides down the hall and shows me to him. Today he is resting in a private room. The bed is against the wall and it feels like a cupboard. The light is stark and I wonder why dimmer switches don't exist in hospitals.

I touch his shoulder and he stirs from his hibernation, very gently opening his eyes. Ten fresh, metal staples clamp the opening in his head shut. It takes him a long moment to recognise me. When he does, he lets out the purest murmurings of consolation and relief, noises he used to comfort me with as a child if I came to him with an injury. Although, this time Dad is wounded.

Something has been taken from him; he looks so frail. The sheets around him are crumpled. I take his hand and notice how tender and supple the skin feels. He looks at me, exhales and closes his eyes. I stay with him and watch a film on my iPad until visiting hours end.

She will be the one who comes

Dad has been moved into a male ward, filled with five other patients. The room feels a bit like a launderette or youth hostel kitchen, a space where strangers are forced to congregate and exchange pleasantries while they wait. However, a shared ward also seems to bring about a great sense of camaraderie as ailment alliances are formed between the patients. The backless gown uniform is a leveller. It's hard to have much of an ego when at any moment, you could find yourself being publicly examined by a group of young doctors or nurses. Outside visiting hours, the wards can either be deathly quiet or patients can chat for hours, share newspapers, gossip about the doctors and pass around photos on their phones.

Anna has come with me. She is the perfect antidote to this situation. She is the kind of person who can feel all the empathy in the world but take the piss out of you three seconds later. The type of person who reminds you that strength around death doesn't have to mean bravery, hushed voices and unending patience. It can be loud, and you can tease, perform, prod, prank, sing, tickle and do anything that occurs to you to bring the fun back into someone's life. Because if you have the strength to shine light into the dark moments, you can provide solace.

All the green curtains around each bed are drawn back and the fluorescent bulbs buzz. In the far-left corner is a skinny, pale man, slumped halfway down the bed, his knees tucked, and his blueish feet pressed against the footboard. He's so thin you can see the outline of his bones under his skin. If he coughed, dust and moths would probably fly out of his mouth. He's staring up at the panelled ceiling. In the opposite corner is an empty bed. Two grey men in their seventies lie silently in the middle beds. They're both sporting large beards and bellies and are both on their phones. They almost look like brothers. In the nearest bed to the right is a small man asleep in a ball, his outline lost amongst the turquoise sheets. I can just about make out his face, hidden beneath a patchy beard. And opposite him, sat upright, is Mr Bump, trying to decipher a magazine. Dad speaks gently and a little incoherently. Asking how we're doing, he holds Anna's hand and deflects any real questions about himself.

I pull out a bag of wine gums and notice the moth man in the corner immediately look up. Slowly walking over to him, I extend the packet but pull it away as he reaches out. His eyes widen with confusion. Teasing, I extend again, before retracting. I then tip half of the pack onto his chest. What then follows can only be described as the most epic and probably inappropriate game of "wine gum toss" ever attempted in a ward. I stand in the centre of the room and fling the sweets at each of the men's gaping mouths. As you would expect there's quite a commotion. The sleeping man in the corner awakens and like a seal, immediately flings himself from one side of his bed to the other. I bring out a chair to get a bit of height and we enter the next level of difficulty. Wine gums in eyes, lost in bed sheets and very few in mouths. A hush falls and the game halts when the nurses wheel in a new chap. As Anna and I say our goodbyes and walk towards the exit, we hear a low hum of chatter as everyone begins to introduce themselves to the new patient.

Bev collects us and we drive to Pond Cottage. Upon arrival, I see plastic pipes and Tops Tiles cardboard packaging leaning against the car port. She hasn't told me about these alterations. We walk in as two young, smiley builders shuffle past. One of them has a tattoo of a pair of red lips on his neck. I look past them and see an almost complete downstairs shower in the utility room. Mounted on the wall is one of those ugly metal hand bars you see in disabled loos. The kind that signals frailty. It upsets me that something so small can signal so much.

"Smart!" yells Anna.

Op successful. Still not sure how much of the "fluffy" stuff was tumour vs radio necrosis.

Rod in pain – can manage that.
Confirmation that current treatment has stopped working and cancer spreading (was always going to happen). It's been 14 months of treatment before there was evidence the tumour returned – that's double the average.

2 x options for alt chemotherapy:
1. PC – 50/50 for 6-9 months. Once every 6 weeks by injection.
2. Avastin – infusion for 30 minutes every 2 weeks (new side effect likely). Can cause hypertension – elevated pressure in the arteries, increase risk of deep vein thrombosis (blood clots), leaky kidneys. This option higher risk, possible positive response. Seen as experimental.

11 Dec next MRI.

15 Dec results.

Rod home. Disoriented, unable to judge distances, very
unsteady during the night, incontinent, restless, agitated, very
weak, head swollen, big headaches.

Oh my God, what a pain in the arse!

Having Dad back home permanently means I am now commuting from Farnham. Bev commutes two days a week with me and despite her munching on her pungent kimchi breakfast pot, I'm grateful for her company. The train is always packed, so the amount of intimate chat between us is limited. But I know she hates leaving him. Most mornings she's got red eyes from crying. She'll tell me why, though, she's straight like that. She'll tell me if Dad pisses the bed or didn't sleep till 5am. Grasses on him when he's been vain about what he will and won't wear and she talks to me when she's struggling. It's hardest when he asks her not to go; it breaks her heart. But she knows Dad's salary isn't enough to cover the mortgage and bills and whatever else might be coming.

It's Friday and I'm home by 8pm, earlier than usual. He's already in bed, sat upright. I take a small run-up and leap towards him as if I'm about to body-slam him. His look of terror is the reason I do it. Every night I spend time with him, discussing the day's goings on. I leave his room and walk into the bathroom opposite. On the windowsill above the bath, there are three soggy candles, an Imperial Leather soap used down to its small centre sticker and a stiffened Big Mouth Billy Bass grinning at me. I push back the crispy shower curtain and run the bath until there's no more hot water. Lying there pretending I'm a crocodile, my nose the only thing out of the water.

I hear Bev walk past into their room. I know she is talking about something serious because Dad's noises have become short and deep.

"Unh-uh!" his favourite interjection.

Then comes shouting, not the kind I am used to – this is more of desperation. Dad in despair, shouting in defence, Bev rational and pleading.

I start trying to guess what it's about before the tone changes as he tries to get out of bed. I hear concern and a small clatter as something falls from a bedside table, then a louder crash as their bathroom door opens and bangs against the wall. Bev yells "Fred!" and I leap from the bath, soaking wet, grab a towel and rush into the room. There, wedged uncomfortably between the sink and the loo, is Dad.

He smiles. We try not to laugh as we grab both arms and yank him free.

I've got a pocket in my vojalais

Bev looks so tired. We clamber into the car and head into town. It takes about the same amount of time to heat the Nissan as it takes to get there. As we get out, Dad turns serious.

"We need to plan for things not going the way we want."

I'm surprised by his fluency.

We walk slowly. Occasionally, I act as a bumper when he starts to lean left and roam off the pavement into the road. Passing Robert Dyas, I wish it was one of those kinds of trip into town. Inside the Nationwide, the grey-and-red patterned carpet makes my eyes fizz. A young manager, whose uniform matches the carpet, stands at a lectern and gives me a pile of Joint Bank Account forms to sign. "On the death of one of the account holders, the account balance passes in its entirety, by the 'principle of survivorship', to the surviving account holder," it reads. I'll now be able to withdraw and access money without him being there, the manager chirpily explains. Dad chips in. "If I die, this will make things easy."

Half the queue turn their heads and look us up and down. I take the forms and don't ask any questions.

Pencil full of lead

At work, I'm developing campaign ideas for KA, the juice company, with black cartons and luminous fonts. Work is a great distraction but at the same time it feels negligent to take my eyes off Dad.

On the opposite corner of Hoxton Square is a tiny Italian café called Rosa's. My boss, Dave, normally takes people there to hire or fire them. Five days ago, a lunch invitation was put into my calendar.

Today, I am sitting opposite Dave, a friendly Scottish man with frameless glasses, wondering whether I'm to be hired or fired. His initial efforts at small talk are awkward, but then he suddenly offers me a full-time job, at a salary of £21K a year. I accept immediately, overjoyed that I don't have to ride the design intern circuit.

As Dave orders two celebratory Arrabiatas, I decide in that moment against telling him anything about Dad.

I'm living with you as hard as I can

For the first time, I accompany Dad and Bev to the Marsden Hospital in Sutton. It feels like an important one. I feel a pang of guilt that I haven't accompanied them earlier, as Bev explains they've tried every sandwich on the little café's menu.

It's different inside from other hospitals – perhaps it's the nine-foot real Christmas tree, or perhaps they use a different bleach. The three of us walk up a long corridor lined with framed art from local schools and ivy-green tinsel. Outside Dr Patrick's office, we are greeted by a receptionist wearing a mechanised reindeer hat. He asks us to wait. Patrick is younger than I had imagined. Late-thirties, with a neat centre parting and round glasses. He's dressed in a bleach white shirt and wears it well.

Dad is holding hands with both of us. Patrick is measured and impossible to read. He is the kind of man who knows how much hope a smile could give, how much fear a frown could stir. His face is deadpan as he goes over his notes. I begin to think how hardened Bev and Dad must be by these appointments. Finally, Patrick delivers his opinion:

"Having no previous post-surgery MRI to compare these results to makes it hard to be conclusive, but judging from my fifteen years of experience, I would say the new treatment is working. It has been halted." Dad squeezes our hands tightly and I watch him close his eyes. Bev slowly tilts her head onto his shoulder and relaxes her back.

"The biggest effect is always seen in the first cycle of treatment and can be effective for up to two years in some patients. Get one more dose in before Christmas and plan a summer holiday."

There it is, a grin from Patrick. I shake his hand last and thank him.

"Your next MRI is booked for 22/23 January. Happy Christmas."

You're my strengthy lady

Bev has spent the entire morning trying to figure out who Oscar is. Whoever he is, Dad wants to call him. I give up after "O-s-c" revealed no clues in his phone. What started as a casual request is now a noisy battle of linguistics and names. She's tried ringing round, checking his work phone and spent 45 minutes locating his old Rolodex.

Sophie has adopted the persona of Hercule Poirot. She's googling anyone who worked at Sony with that name – there are seven Oscars and none of them right. She's now carefully taking him through his work phone contacts one name at a time. If there's an Oscar to be found these two will find him. There isn't. Poirot solves the case when her finger hovers above "Sally". Dad presses dial and smiles.

I will ask you to blow some of the house away

My earliest memory is of lying on my dad's stomach as he slept in one Wandsworth morning. He was wearing a zebra-stripped, towelled dressing gown and I can remember the feeling of the fabric on my cheek. His breathing was heavy, slow and ceaseless, like an elephant's. I tried holding my breath to see if I could match it, but never could.

It's Christmas Day, and we've all opened our presents and eaten lunch. Dad and I are lying on a sofa in the snug in a comatose state. The blinds are down, a pile of used ribbons lie neatly coiled, ready to be recycled for next year's presents and Soph is working her way through an entire pack of firelighters to get the fire going. The room's warped door is ajar and through it I can see Bev as she potters around the Welsh dresser. The laden tree bends into the ceiling and looks ridiculous in the little room. The metal of the wood burner ticks as it starts to heat up. I change positions and use Dad's belly as a pillow. He is asleep, his lips flapping every time he breathes out. I match my breathing with his. Submerging into the safety of that moment, I slip into the most peaceful sleep.

Hot, red face – no temperature though.

Head surgery wound looks infected.

R has weakness (dead weight) with an inability to sit up – likely caused by Avastin.

Confusion and words very jumbled.

Occasional incontinence.

Lower back aches.

Steroids likely to make R gain weight.

25 January 2013

Blood pressure is up.

Some parts of MRI scan look slightly worse.

Treatment's effectiveness slowing.

Rod seems well himself. Scan in 6 weeks after 1 more cycle to calculate rate of deterioration. Then some serious conversations about next steps.

Sophie will be told after her GCSEs.

28 January 2013

Collect wheelchair from Red Cross.
Blood clots identified in lungs.

Give me beddy snooze

It's pouring with rain as I cycle from Waterloo to East London, so I dive into a Tesco and grab two carrier bags to tie around my feet. I look deranged and soggy as I walk into the subterranean studio where I work. At one end of the basement there is a wall of windows where you can see people walking above on the pavement. The basement was previously used for dance classes, so a huge wall of mirrors hangs on the opposite end, acting as a daily reminder that underground office life makes you paler.

Dad calls just before lunch. My socks are still drying on the radiator and my feet pad loudly on the wooden floor as I go to pick up.

He sounds panicked. "Where are you?"

"I'm at work."

"When are you coming home?"

Almost embarrassed: "Normal time, Dad."

I then hear Dad yelling for Bev. There is rustling at the end of the line as she comes on.

"He's very agitated today."

"Where is he?" Dad asks in the background again.

She then levels with me: "We've entered a new phase."
Everything else in my life just got deprioritised. A hot feeling
traps itself under my diaphragm. I ask Dave if I can speak
to him upstairs in private. We find an empty office and he
closes the door. I crumble, barely able to get the words out.
Three minutes ago, we were discussing typefaces and now
I'm trying to explain the full extent of the last 17 months.

"Go and we'll work something out."

I'm flushed with relief. I knew this day was coming and
there's no alternative. I need to be with him. Bev wants
Sophie and me there too; she knows he'll be calmer with his
children around him. I cannot comprehend how much time
he has left; it feels untethered from any tangible notion of
days, weeks, months. If I lose my job, I've got some savings
to see me through.

Arriving home, I find Dad sitting by the glass patio doors
in a tall, heavily cushioned armchair. He greets me with great
anguish, says nothing and points towards the snug. Both
sofas have been moved out and two men in blue are assem-
bling something inside. I walk into the room and see the
beige metal frame of a Solite Pro Electric hospital bed. The
head and foot of the bed are plastic with a printed wood
effect, and there are wheels on each leg and a remote sealed
in a wipe-clean plastic wrap dangling from one side. As the
mattress is brought in, I turn to see Dad, doggedly staggering
up the stairs.

You are the right person to be my person

Sophie and I have borrowed Dad's dressing gowns and are pretending to be WWE wrestlers. I sit in the corner of his bedroom and announce the next challenger. She approaches, stomping her feet down the corridor.

"Weighing in at less than 100lb, making her the lightest fighter to ever grace this cottage, ladies and gentlemen, I give you featherweight champion of the world, Sophie."

She bellows and pounces on Dad. The fight is over in a matter of moments. Sophie has pulled up his T-shirt and administered the most enormous raspberry. Instant win. My turn. Now traditionally, Dad never wins, but he does normally put up a bit of a fight. In a flash I'm upon him, grab his arms and wait for the resistance. The skin around his biceps is loose and his strength isn't there. His face says he's trying but I can't believe he is. I feign being overpowered by him, pretend to pull a muscle and wait for a reaction. Slowly he rises and bear-hugs me, pulling me in, before delivering the coup-de-grace, a wet raspberry to my cheek. The fight is over.

A rare win for the old man.

In the afternoon, we drive to Frensham Pond, a large lake surrounded by felled woodland. On the far side, about half a mile from the car park, is a sailing club. Toppers dart across the water. The beach at the north end looks as if it had been imported from the Caribbean. Dad finds it hard to walk across, his feet unstable, his ankles sore and shaky. We make it to the hard soil path past the sand and spy anglers on the dark banks under trees that drape above the water. Dogs speed past and all three of us feel Dad's unease. It's getting dark already and he's fumbling his words, angry, then soft, then drained. I jog back to the car and collect a black folded wheelchair. It's heavy and cold. I decide to carry it across the sand, unfold it on the path and wheel it towards them. Reluctantly and tentatively, he approaches the chair. He forces down the bottom fabric, testing its strength, turns his back to it and with the help of all three of us, sits. He's exhausted and says very little as we push him. He keeps checking to see if his flat cap has fallen off his head, before letting his arms go limp by his sides. This is the first time he has looked conquered.

At home, the promise of banana cake and cups of tea delivered to his armchair has brought back his voice. I play up to the role reversal of caring for my parent and present him with a slice of cake, gliding it towards his mouth. He opens wide and keeps his eyes fixed upon it. Slowly, like a plane diverting course, it heads straight into mine. Mouth shut, yum. The astonishment, the cruelty of it, the jovial cries of protest.

"Happy Birthday, Dad," I say as I stuff a piece into his querulous mouth.

I need the snow harrows

It's early, we're flying to Scotland for a late birthday treat for Dad. The four of us wait outside the lift that takes us to the departure terminal at Gatwick. The doors open and Soph wheels Dad inside. It's the first time Dad has seen himself in a full-length mirror.

"Chubby boy," he exclaims with wide eyes, dumbfounded at how inflated he looks.

Thin, skeleton-like figures come to mind when I think of cancer but the recent increase in steroid dosage means Dad, specifically Dad's face, has ballooned. His eyes are lost between his brows and his cheeks. He's still looking at himself as we wheel him out of the lift and towards check-in.

Perhaps it is the combination of wheelchair, inflated face and fifteen metal staples in the side of his head that draws eyes. Either way I'm shocked by how much people stare. We're last on board the EasyJet flight, all eyes on us. I begin to worry that I'm going to have to ask a kind stranger to help hoist Dad out of his wheelchair. Fortunately, they have removed a seat next to Bev. We park him up and lock his wheels.

By 11am, we're driving out of Edinburgh towards St Andrews West Sands beach, the place we visited for Dad's 60th, two years ago, before he was ill.

We avoid the sand and take turns to push him along the tarmac, through the car park and across the hardened earthy path. Almost a mile and a half away from the city, we spy a rising lip of earth that looks out over the beach. It takes all our strength to tug and yank his wheelchair through the deep sand. The tide is out, the water rests 200 metres away and families, dogs and runners speckle the sand. We spend 40 minutes there, taking photographs of ourselves making the most hideous faces we can think of.

I don't want him having babies without having extra bits

Emily is staying for a few days. I keep thinking what a kind and gentle person she is, but I'm irritated by how lightly she treads, figuratively and literally. She tiptoes around the cottage, careful not to disrupt.

People deal with death in different ways and I'm starting to learn what type I like: the no-bullshit, slightly loud, no-pretending, good-at-distractions kind. Her softness comes from the most loving place but her stillness, hugs and delicate kisses aren't helping. I'm conflicted. What are you supposed to do when this could be the last girlfriend your dad will ever meet?

It's not some approval thing – I just want whoever I spend my life with to have known my dad. There's a context and an understanding. She knows what it's like to be in his presence. She knows how soft his hands are. She knows his nuances, his character. She's spent time with him, knows how tall he is and has seen his tenderness. That might sound naive but it matters and Dad likes Emily a lot. I shrug off my thoughts as she quietly brings me a cup of tea, before going back to her book.

Rod admitted to St George's for CSF* drain procedure,** or more commonly referred to as a "spinal tap". Drain put in.

> *Cerebrospinal Fluid Culture.
> **A physician will insert a needle into the space between two vertebrae in the lower spine. The needle will then be moved carefully into the CSF-filled space surrounding the spinal cord.

Drain removed (was in wrong place).
Drain put in (successfully).

Twelve tickets to the rodeo

Dad calls me into the snug.

"I'd like to donate my head when I die. But I won't do it if you don't want me to."

I've never heard a more brutal sentence.

"Possibly, the worst idea you've ever had."

To be fair, he was close. He confused "head" with "brain", but the image of my headless father in a casket remains. Nobody is taking anything from my dad, no matter what good it might do.

Rod on new pain management course and mobility has improved.
Still refusing downstairs bed. Might need stair rail.
V encouraging to see.

Listening to BBC Radio 4's Great Lives: Henry Cooper then Rasputin.

Blood pressure higher today.

Come on you wonderful wizards

He's chirpy this morning. I pad down the stairs and walk over to the armchair.

"I'd like a milkshake, please," he says, looking up at me.

Bev interjects pointing to the left high-stool. On it is a luminous banana and spinach smoothie. I present it to him, confused myself. Despite this, he continues his request, adamant, almost whining.

Perhaps he's turning total diva. I change into jogging bottoms and walk out the door, intent on getting him what he wants.

There is a Tesco a mile along Shortheath Road. Although I've lived here for twelve years, I've never taken it upon myself to run along this road. It is quintessentially Surrey suburbia. Tall hedgerows politely hiding the mediocre grandeur of the houses from the world. I find a chocolate Frijj and buy a newspaper too.

Dad is waiting expectantly when I come through the door.

I tip the contents of the bag onto his lap. Thanking me, he fumbles for the newspaper.

"Milkshake," he says, shaking the paper as if to say "see" and opens it.

I look at Bev; she glances back at me.

"No, newspaper," I reply.

"Yes, newspaper," he parrots, getting frustrated, clearly unable to hear his tangle. I pour the chocolate shake into a pint glass in front of him, and he puts the newspaper down and asks whether it's for him.

I watch him scanning the broadsheet's pictures, before settling on an article. His eyes stick to single words, unable to move across the line. He looks down and tries again. This time his eyes just aimlessly float and drift. He breathes furiously through his nostrils and opens the sports section. The large photographs distinguish winners from losers. Unhappy managers and cricketers raising their bats. His mood softens as he looks at the photos, asking me only once to read a headline.

Occipital lobe and temporal lobe – vision and speech likely to get much worse. Rod had nosebleed straight after MRI.

Rod struggling to sleep all the way through. Lots of conversations in the night and no understanding of time.

Plop, plop, plop, plop, plop

Generally, people who have had to wipe their parent's arse don't joke about it, and those who have never had the pleasure, do.

Dad is already halfway across the kitchen when I spot him making a bee-line for the loo. Bev is out, so I call to him, asking if he needs me. He bats his free arm away at me, clinging to the worktop with the other. He can't see I'm watching him as he grapples with the support bar, groaning as he does so. He sits down. I go back to whatever I was doing until I hear a loud clattering, then a thud and then shouting. I find him, trousers around his ankles, fallen face first into the wall opposite him. The soap dish is in a thousand pieces and the hand rail is half wrenched out of the wall. I lean him upright and see a nasty cut on the top of his head. The blood has already soaked the shoulders of his T-shirt and there's a grimace on his face. He holds wet tissues to the wound. He's angry. I ask him to bend forward; pulling up his T-shirt, I see a large surgical plaster with yellowish-brown discolouration at the base of his spine. His back is broad and smooth. He shifts forward and I wipe. It feels wrong and demeaning, yet instinctively I do it without getting shit anywhere it shouldn't be. I push him backwards and help him pull up his jeans. He says nothing as he stands, but his eyes are red, watery and look directly into mine. I help him back to the armchair, before running upstairs to fetch a clean T-shirt and plaster, hoping he won't need stitches.

I've never told anyone that story.

Rod to Royal Surrey A+E by ambulance at 22:00
because of prolonged nosebleed. Has to stay overnight.

How's Tracey?

Sophie is downstairs; she's here every weekend, between her school weeks. It is 11am and Dad has been up for three hours. I have been awake for three hours but have chosen to stay away, casual internet surfing taking priority over him. I feel compromised, somewhat bored of the tedium of being at the beck and call of a demanding father but riddled with guilt if I don't go down to help Bev and Sophie. My room sits above the kitchen and the armchair Dad commands from. He has finished his breakfast and I hear him gently ask after me. As Bev approaches my door. and knocks, I pretend to be asleep, before stirring and performing the "just woken" routine. I don't know why I'm doing this. Dad is waiting eagerly for me to arrive as I walk downstairs.

"Hello, brother," he says first, then corrects himself. "Would you mind stuffing my pipe?"

He mimes slapping shaving foam on both cheeks and points to the razor.

I started puberty late, barely own a razor and was never given the father-and-son-standing-in-front-of-the-mirror shaving demonstration, so I feel somewhat underqualified to fulfil the request. Dad straightens his back into the tartan green armchair, places his arms in his lap and lifts his chin to the ceiling. I watched Bev shave him last week and know how much he delights in it.

I act full Italian barber, gliding across the wooden floor in my socks, welcoming him to this most famous of establishments. I introduce myself as Luigi and examine the work to be done.

I take a purple bath towel and tuck it into the neck of his T-shirt before pressing a hot flannel to his face. The customer barks when the steamy cloth scalds him a little. I explain, "It's to open your pores, Signore," before blowing on his face gently. Looking closely, I see just how many grey bristles sprout from Dad's puffy cheeks. Tiny bright-red capillaries net together just under the surface and the skin on his nose looks raw and thinner than ever.

I begin to lather shaving foam in my palms and gently spread it over his cheeks and neck. His pursed lips go pale from being pushed together, his face contorts to maximise coverage and his breathing intensifies as he concentrates. I swap the old blade for a fresh one and activate the vibrating button. With as much precision as I can, I glide the razor down from sideburn towards jawline. He makes concerned noises. Even with the sharpest blade there is still some tugging at his cheeks, and with every movement comes further anguish.

Dad begins to relax as we come to the end. I dip the end of the towel in warm water and wipe away any excess foam, before cleansing all over. He likes this part the most.

He pats both cheeks, checking the quality of the shave. Satisfied, he nods thank you. What he hasn't noticed is the perfect toothbrush moustache I have left. It brings a new level of absurdity to Pond Cottage as Adolf enthroned in his chair asks what he's getting for lunch.

Rod stayed in bed until 11:30. He got up, washed, showered and dressed himself without help.

He refused pain relief but as we are phasing out anti-inflammatory drugs – codeine must be taken.

Concerned back pain is getting worst. Trip to Waitrose, Rod used walking stick only.

Sophie and Freddy don't want any counselling.

Massage tomorrow.

I want him exercised

Bluebell heads in the front garden are just beginning to show, signalling winter is ending. I've started running on the mornings I can be bothered, partly to escape the cottage. At the halfway point there's a forest on a hill. From the top plateau, you can't see much more than from the bottom, but I get the same sense up here as I did inside St Peter's Church in Edinburgh. Scots pine trees and dry dust on the ground give it a wonderfully earthy smell. You can't hear the road and I like how alone I feel. Up here, I'm free to breathe and barter some more. It's helping.

Rod resisting physio exercises to help mobility and back pain. He feels it is too cold for Norwegian therapy – it's very cold outside though!

5pm district nurse injection.
He's not hungry – has only eaten a banana today.

Fire the gazebo

Dad has just finished lunch and is positioned comfortably in the snug. He can answer simple questions and understands exactly what we're saying, but the difficulty comes when he wants to express himself separately from an existing conversation.

"Can we get naked bread?" he asks.

I'm sitting on a sofa in the open-plan area across from him. I can see him if I turn and look around the partition in the wall. He's not distressed but distracted by the numerous crumbs on his napkin. I have my iPad in front of me and I'm about to start watching another film. This will be my third of the day so far. I'd rather spend time with Hollywood than with the most important man I know. I'd rather escape into something entertaining and inane than ask him questions I know I will want the answers to someday. He isn't beyond answering them; we'd struggle but we'd get there. I am not asking those questions as to do so would be to confront a finality I'm not ready for. And where do I start? Instead of opening Pandora's box, I'd rather sit in a room next door than beside him and remind him how much

I care. The deeper I go, the more unable to move I become. I feel like some benign cyst, a useless sac filled with fluid. I am wasting the most precious time but cannot help myself. Not everybody gets an opportunity to ask their parents about the things that matter. Dad's not reticent and would answer anything. What did you do when your dad died? Do you wish you'd had Sophie and me earlier? How do I be a good dad? What's important? When were you happiest? Why the car rides of silence? How did you cope with being fired from your job, the day before you married Mum? What are your eight tracks, book and luxury? What do you wish you'd done more of? Regrets? Advice? Memories? I might know some of these answers already, but I could cast them in metal in my mind. All I have to do is get up. I have been gifted this opportunity, so get up, Fred. But instead, I squander it with Adam Sandler. I loathe myself.

MRI back results at Royal Marsden. Bottom of spine is disintegrating. Needs to be operated on.

Rod moved to St George's for operation tomorrow.

Clear liquid leaking from stomach scar.
Spinal consultation on the 24th.

Palliative care team – ready when necessary.

Rod very sleepy all day, sedative at night.

Increase Dex. (steroid) to 6mg for 3 days then drop to 1-2mg if improvement in speech/cognition.

It's up to me

I wake up early to hear Dad talking coherently downstairs. I listen hard. He hasn't sounded like this for months. He's chatting to a day nurse about her family, politely declining any more breakfast and asking whether he has had all his medication. Buoyant, Dad greets me with a fluency which he is obviously relishing. He's sharp and tells me I should get out of my pyjamas and kindly give him a shave. "No dictators this time, please!" he shouts after me as I take the stairs three at a time.

Open on my laptop is an article about dichloroacetate (DCA) from *Nature*, a weekly scientific journal. It's about the resurgence of the drug and its effects on shrinking or slowing tumours, particularly glioblastoma. I spent a lot of last week googling for answers, for hope. The article states that a team studied tumour samples from 49 patients with glioblastoma and found that all of them had an altered mito-chondrial function that could be reversed by DCA. Mito-chondrial function is a cell's ability to convert the energy from food into a form they can use. I keep reading. The team then treated five patients with it for fifteen months, before comparing their tumour tissue to tissue before treatment. In all, there were signs that the tumour growth had slowed, and more cancer cells were undergoing programmed cell death after the treatment with DCA.

I sprint towards the shower, turn on the pump and stand under the dribbly low pressure. This article and Dad's fluency give me two positives to hold onto. Something has happened to him overnight and this is day one of recovery. Finally, his back is better and like a chain reaction, his strength to fight is returning. And then there are the American trials and DCA and the answer. I fantasise, feeling full of hope, until my fingers prune and I spring out of the shower.

– Commode on wheels (can be used as internal wheel-chair)

– Slide sheet (will help move him and push up bed)

– Ramp

Jock and Mongie call with details, they'll help with money.

Had to be realistic with Freddy.

Rod's brothers visiting.

Who else is on this ferry?

"I feel so old." Dad exhales fluently from his armchair.

All three of us look towards him and see him looking into a hand mirror. Moments like these are now a daily occurrence for my dad, but I've never heard him quite so eloquently low. I squat next to him and press my face against his until we share the mirror.

"Not surprised, when you're sporting a mullet like that, Dad. You might be balding at the top but there's a party happening around the back."

Within two hours and on a Sunday, Bev has managed to find Carl, a part-time hairdresser, part-time professional weightlifter. I watch a man with biceps bigger than my thighs trim Dad's hair with such delicate care. Despite this visual absurdity, Dad relaxes into the ordinariness of this small ritual and for the rest of the day feels a little younger.

Lorazepam can offset anxiety and help relax – try using rather than sleeping aid. Good sleep can become your best weapon.

Rod massage 12:30-13:00.

Could be issues with swallowing safety in future. Feeding tubes means lots of discomfort, would only recommend for treatable patients. Not using it doesn't mean patient starves to death, other causes will come first.

Rare to die of respiratory failure from tumour. CT scan showed growth of it, causing pressure.
Need to consider we are at the beginning of last stages.

Rod massage 16:30-17:00.

Jeweller coming tomorrow to talk about Sophie's 16th birthday present.

Please don't take her away

Sophie finished her final GCSE exam yesterday. Five days ago, she turned sixteen. She came straight here and slept downstairs next to Dad. Today is the day he wants me to tell her. She knows it is bad, she's knows it is cancer, she knows it is in his head, but she hasn't been told the full truth and it falls to me to break it to her.

After breakfast, I ask her if she can come with me into the garden. The stone patio is surrounded by Bev's wild herbs, and we brush past lavender, rosemary, sage and loads more I don't know. The garden is looking neglected; the wooden outdoor furniture, once B&Q orange, is now green and slippery to the touch. Large ceramic pots, some empty, some cracked, some waiting to be replanted with bulbs, sit against the wooden wall of the car port. A tiny step with grass clenching its edges takes you to uncut lawn. I think about how many woodlice are under it.

Our bare feet are already damp before we get to the small damson tree. There, out of earshot, I begin to explain. I can't control my voice. I think of Sophie as the baby bum-shuffler I grew up with, whose world I am about to obliterate. She has one dad and I am about to tell her that he won't be here for her exam results in August. It has to be me to tell her.

As one of her pillars crumbles, I have to stand straighter and stronger than ever.

It is the most terrible conversation. Her fear and disbelief transform the way she looks at me. Through ferocious and suffocating sobs, she inhales, repeating three words again and again: "This is mad." She pulls away from me and runs into the house, sprinting past Dad, up to her room. I watch him helplessly try to get up from his armchair. He calls out but it comes out like a whisper. He keeps saying her name, his voice softening as he begins to plead and beg.

I sit down on a moth-eaten tartan rug on the grass and watch Dad try to stand, still saying, "Sophie?"

One lumbue please

A pain in my throat wakes me up. My sheets are sodden with sweat and I can't swallow. I can hear Dad talking to the night nurse. The landing is impossible to walk across quietly. My search for water lets Dad know someone is awake upstairs. He calls out. I tread quietly downstairs towards the snug. He's naked, sat upright, using his commode. The angel-like night nurse busies herself around him, helping and guiding. My throat is throbbing so much I can barely speak. Wrapping my arms around Dad's smooth back and squeezing, I ask whether I could borrow a thermometer. Dad and I are quite the pair, shitting and sweating side by side.

By 10am I resemble Mark Renton going cold turkey and Bev drops me off at A&E. I'm examined and told I've got 40 throat and mouth ulcers. "Are you stressed at the moment?" the A&E doctor asks me kindly. Using my phone's flash and a mirror in a hospital bathroom, I can see a wall of white behind my tongue. I spray the back of my throat with the numbing agent I've been prescribed and switch off my phone. I feel exhausted. I want to appear stoic and strong. I want to be a merrymaker to keep Bev's and Sophie's spirits up. I want to distract them from the juggernaut approaching. I want to keep the roof up with all the fun I can muster, but my body is suffering. My left eye has a small yellow lesion on it, the skin is raised red and angry on the left side of my chest and I count four new verrucas on my feet. I'm admitted to a ward, put on a drip and told I'll have to stay overnight.

Surprisingly, I find an affinity for cardboard urine containers – never have I known a better convenience.

Will speak to Phyllis Tuckwell nurses about helping me counsel Rod better.

Hospice at home coming at 4pm.

I miss the conversation of intelligent people

Today Dad's answer to everything is the East African country, Zambia.

"Where's Zambia gone?" "Two Zambias please." "I'd like to put some Zambia on that." "Who has my Zambia?" "My Zambia hurts." "Can someone change my Zambia? "Hello, Zambia? "I Zambia you." "Time for Zambia, I think." "I need to call Zambia." "Can you switch on the Zambia?" "Zambia?" "Zambia!" "Zambia."

It's actually quite straightforward to translate. When daily requests rarely go off script, you can quickly predict what's being requested. Except for "Who has my Zambia?" That one was tricky.

I'll have a sugar sausage, please

A letter arrived in the post today marked "To be opened by Freddy" in Mum's handwriting. Inside is a letter for Dad that she'd like me to read to him. I read it through myself first and am already crying by the second sentence. It speaks of a shared life. Of ten years of love, of holidays, of Acris Street, of happiness. That everything will be taken care of. A letter that asks nothing. A private conversation I get to listen to. Just an old friend, saying all that needs to be said and mending what needs mending.

"Dad, I've got a letter from Mum here for you."

He looks up and smiles.

Hard luck, lard arse

An enthusiastic spectator of sport, Dad would berate and shout at the television until his own children were scared. Standing at the actual sidelines of a pitch, he was even louder. On one occasion, at an Under-9s game of mine, he was shown a red card and asked to leave for abusing the referee.

Today, Murray is playing Djokovic in the Wimbledon final, and Dad is the most agitated he's been all summer. He's pulling at his clothes, refusing porridge and repeating "Is it now?" over and over again. He is worry personified, shifting anxiously within his armchair at the thought of an unfavourable outcome.

When it begins, he's transfixed, continually uttering unintelligible groans and shouts, feeling every moment, as if the result would directly affect his own life. He keeps asking me how it's going. It's going well. He seems able only to gauge the broader picture and can't follow the commentary. As the game progresses, Dad's agitations start to consume him and he asks to be taken outside to the garden and we have to shout minute-by-minute updates out to him.

Match over, Murray is the victor. Dad in his sun lounger

is euphoric, ecstatic, drenched in sweat and shaking the nurse's hands as if he personally had thrashed Novak.

For the rest of the afternoon, he is victorious. For now, thoughts of yellow balls, grass and trophies distract him from tomorrow's routine anxiety and his own future. We are so grateful. Fuck knows what'll happen if England lose the Ashes next week, though.

It's so hurt and so soft

Tonight, there is a book launch for a group of photographers in the gallery above my office. I leave the cottage bunker and make the trip into London, arriving to cava and canapés. I struggle to make conversation and use the excuse of last trains to leave early. Life here hasn't stopped. The Red Lion is still overflowing, people are still dancing downstairs in Electricity Showroom, the number 35 is still running and I'm jealous I can't join in.

It's 2am by the time I'm home. All the lights are off. Leaving my shoes at the door, I tiptoe quietly through the kitchen. Flashing red chilli lights dangle above the windows. Passing the dining table, I spy the snug door is half open. Dad calls out Bev's name, his voice reaching out through the dark. I make out the look of relief on Dad's face when he realises someone can hear him.

"Ahh, hello, hello!" Almost shouting with excitement, he calls me inside. Next to Dad is an empty single bed with a sheet on it. Bev has been sleeping next to him every night since he moved downstairs, but tonight, desperate for some rest, she's upstairs. He listens so intently as I tell him about my evening. Before I disappear, he asks me not to close the door all the way. As I leave the room, I watch him silently in the darkness. He can't see me. He blows out his cheeks, exhales an anxious breath and casts his eyes wide above. Upstairs in my bedroom, I can hear him talking to himself. I listen to his quiet panic, suffering in silence so as not to wake anyone up. I grab my duvet and join him in the snug.

The biggest sky

The girls have gone to do the weekly shop and the day nurse is making Dad some pasta. I've brought my laptop down and have it resting open on his tummy. I explain to him I'd like to do a recording of him for Sophie. His eyes moisten at the request. He knows what he's being asked to do; whether he's able is another matter.

"I thought you could sing 'Sunshine' for her."

He nods, I press record and count him in.

"You are my s…."

He stops, unable to remember the words. He tries again but can't get past the first line. I sing it for him. If I can just get individual words, I can cobble it together on software afterwards.

"Sundine. Moontime. Sunshine."

Got it. He then sings the second line with more fluidity, first time. Now the third.

"You'll make me Sophie, to take my Sophie away."

He tries again but can't differentiate lines. "Sophie" has become lodged in his head as the central lyric and he's beginning to get very distressed that he can't fulfill this simple request for his daughter.

"You'll never Sophie Sophie how much I Sophie."

I keep pushing, trying new ways to get him to parrot me. I try mouthing, I try playing the original song, I try the King's Speech approach, plugging his ears with music. Nothing is working and now he's crying. Enough.

"We'll try tomorrow, Dad."

"OK," he replies, not looking up.

I know I've missed my opportunity. I should have seized the moment months ago, but instead I let time drift by. My self-loathing drops through the floor as I try editing a patch-work of lyrics together into some semblance of the song and realise I'm missing the whole last two lines.

Lying on my bedroom floor, I do the only thing I can think of: I turn on the microphone and whisper the last two lines myself.

15 July 2013

Mark visiting at 10:00
Julia visiting at 11:30
13:00 massage
Rod very emotional after Ashes win.

Glug, glug, glug

Wednesday afternoon. Tamsyn, a university friend, gave me two hours' notice and drove straight from London to Pond Cottage. She pulls up in her new, second-hand convertible, blue Mazda MX5. Roof down.

"Jump in, where to?"

Frensham Ponds for swimming, then the Bat and Ball for dinner. We sink four pints each and a jug of Pimms, then decide to return to the ponds for a night-time dip. It's raining hard and the sky is starless. As she enters the water a flash of lightning illuminates her and the forest surrounding the water. She looks beautiful. Like some kind of silver, fleeting companion. For the first time in a long time, Pond Cottage leaves my head and I'm so grateful to her for that. She stays the night but is up before breakfast, leaving before the day nurses start their shift.

Dwayne Jasset

A palliative care duo scrub Dad in the downstairs shower room. This morning, I'm awoken by noises of laughing and flirting as two angels clean between his toes.

Yesterday, it was the opposite. Yelling, fierce anger, confusion and the sound of metal clattering met with soft but stern instructions. His reaction to the nurses' soapy intrusion becomes our morning radio show, dictating his mood for the day.

All three of them smile at me as I poke my head around the door. He's naked, slouched atop a commode. They dry his middle, carefully avoiding the stitches below his stomach. He looks like a bear being pampered.

Once in his armchair, his spirit keeps rising. Singing out to us, "My fish is in the toaster." Vaguely gazing towards said (empty) toaster, I'm completely stumped. Bev, however, has mastered this indiscernible language. She opens the patio doors and brings his slippers in from outside. Cinderella grins as Sophs places them on his feet.

The phone rings. Bev scrambles for the handset, then freezes. I spy the cause: Dad's got the phone, his finger poised above the green button. Up until this point, we have been standing in as full-time translators for helpless visiting friends or family. It takes concentration and is normally fairly unsuccessful. Now Dad is on the brink of a phone call catastrophe. Anyone could be calling: his GP, surgeon, the Royal Marsden, NatWest, his work, his lawyer. Dad might not be able to communicate but he can understand exactly what he's being told. He is delicate, and one bit of hard-hitting truth is enough to make him spiral. We brace as he presses green.

"Hello...?"

We can't believe it. He seems to be having a normal conversation, albeit one-sided, he makes the right sounds, chuckling when appropriate. He tries asking a question but gets in a muddle and tells the caller to ignore him. I hear a series of short muffled questions that he answers with a simple "yes" or "no". I stand beside him and try and figure out who is on the other end. No clues. Astonishingly, he begins to wrap it up. "Yes, yes, I'll pass you over."

Gobsmacked, Bev asks, "Who is it?"

"Dwayne Jasset," he replies confidently, passing Bev the phone.

It's his friend Louise on the line. We fall about laughing, as he looks on innocently.

You're the winner and I'm a winner

Brilliant sunshine scorches the wicket of Shackleford cricket pitch. The charred black pavilion is suffering badly from subsidence and it takes me fifteen minutes to wheel Dad up the slope towards it. For 20 years he has hosted matches here, but today he is staring blankly as I lock his wheels just behind the boundary rope. This is his testimonial match.

He refuses to move onto the cushions and rugs, as we set up an assortment of umbrellas to shade him. Sophie takes up position as chief fan attendant, ensuring optimum temperature is maintained. Dad resembles a stewed red onion by the time every friend available has arrived.

Last month, I had hopes of him playing a mischievous umpire. Instead, he's 80 metres from the action, soaked in sweat and visibly overcome everytime he recognises an old friend coming for a hug.

Sometime during the second innings, he misses the mark with his plastic urine collector and covers himself in piss. He's sticky and upset so Bev decides to take him home. We halt the match. His friends, dressed in dusty cricket whites, stand in two lines, creating a guard of honour and erupting into a huge noise as he is pushed towards the car. No amount of whooping and cheering can distract me from his face and his hysterical crying.

Don't put yourself on toast

I remember in school when I was very young, playing the game "what would you rather lose: your sight or your hearing?" I would cover my eyes first, then place my hands over my ears, trying to imagine life without one or the other. I always chose to keep my sight.

I can see Dad in the snug. He's enjoying listening to an audiobook. The same question comes to me, except this time with a plethora of options to choose from. Which would you rather see him lose? His vision? Hearing? Memories? Taste? Touch? Smell? Speech? Recognition? He has to lose one in this lottery of impairments. Now choose.

I think about it for a long time, imagining him unable to recognise his family, or unable to produce words, or completely paralysed, or overcome by seizures, or developing a new personality, or unable to see or hear, unable to remember, to understand, to swallow, to keep his head up or to even breathe. Then I begin to feel something I haven't felt for a long time, and that is lucky. He might speak in muddled riddles and sometimes it feels like we're living with a mature exchange student and it's beyond hard work, but it's nothing in comparison to what it could have been.

His loss of one kind of cognition has strengthened his ability to express himself in other ways. He's more emotionally in tune than I've ever known him to be. His dysphasia has given him sentences with the power to break us up into a million pieces. Nonsensical expressions that somehow went beyond the levels of love I've ever heard expressed. Outbursts that made us laugh when we didn't think we could. Whispers that punctured the dark. And phrases capable of turning idle Tuesdays into days I'll never forget.

I need nothing more than a celebration to say you are kings and queens

Another casserole was left on our doorstep this morning. Yesterday we were drowning in charity bolognese as three separate individuals silently gifted it. Today, more visitors are scheduled, and I start picturing how each might respond to Dad's state. The worst is when he needs to pee while they are here and all dignity vanishes as a nurse or Bev whips off his trousers and pants.

The best visitors are those that come often, check before and don't outstay. They don't pretend to understand what we're going through but instead level with us and tell us how utterly shit it is. They're dependable, they pick up their phones, they take us out and stay the night.

Call me on the hot number

He isn't showering this morning. The cottage is quiet. Wearing boxers and one of Dad's oversized T-shirts, I go downstairs and enter the snug. A throne of pillows surrounds him. A double duvet and two woollen quilts are tucked under his sides. It's hard to imagine how you could make someone more comfortable. I feel his hand, which is cold despite it being a summer's day and all his coverings. He looks up into my face, understands who he's looking at and lets out a long, relieved sigh.

"My brother, my brother."

I don't correct him.

"Good morning, Dad."

Wonderful, wonderful

I was once told it would be like it is for a field mouse in winter. Without burrows, nests or houses to protect them, the tiny creatures slip gently into an unbreakable sleep. As their core temperature drops, they stop eating and become drowsy as their body begins to shut down. They then sleep, feeling no pain as they drift away.

Rod asleep.
Breathing is interrupted by gasping.

Come on, you bastard

He isn't waking up. Deep, long breath in, his lips flap like a horse when the air is forced out. Again and again.

Bev brings a glass of water to his mouth and trickles some inside. He chokes immediately, spluttering water down his chin. He doesn't open his eyes; he doesn't wake up. Sophie brings a cold soaked flannel to his lips and he gently sucks on it. I am not ready to comprehend what's happening. I begin to shake him, cheerily at first, but then with more force and vigour as my panic sets in. I hit his belly, trying to summon the power of a defibrillator. I quietly yell his name, each time getting closer to his face until Bev tugs me away. I try and remember what our last exchange was. I'm panicking. I walk out into the garden. It's night-time and I can hear the rumble of cars on Shortheath Road. I feel hollowed out at the thought of never being able to have another conversation with him. I need to call someone who can help, so I call Anna.

I'm leaping the loop

Paul Simon's *Graceland*, as high as the dial allows, blasts throughout the cottage. "The Mississippi Delta was shining like a national guitar", Dad's favourite lyric, sticks in my head. The three of us are there beside him, in the snug.

Cancel tree surgeons.

Oh how far we could have gone. We would have done it in style

The hearse pulls up outside Pond Cottage. On the opposite side of Shortheath Road is a shady green funeral home. We had intentionally avoided using them.

Sophie, Bev and I climb into the back of a smart black Mercedes E-class. The last time I was in the back of one of these was when I accidentally requested an UberLUX. We don't speak as the procession drives towards Guildford Crematorium. It's only when approaching Europe's largest roundabout that I begin to regret not putting more thought into our route. Friday traffic whips pasts us, taking no notice of the care and respect we deserve. We're about to join the A31. Christ.

I think about Wednesday morning school runs with him. I think about Crondall Lane and the dense tunnel of ash trees, whose branches entwined above the road. I know how much he loved it when trees make those leafy canopies. The one I have in my head is about half a mile long. I daydream about our line of black cars rolling under it, as yellow fields of rape flash past between the trunks: the peace of it all.

A loud honking brings me back to the A31. A red Renault Megane has driven in between us and the hearse, and our driver is visibly distressed. I can't see Dad. I can only see two arseholes, oblivious to their faux pas. They exit our lane and we pass them. They're aware of their mistake but can't keep the grins off their faces. The bastards.

We arrive. I spy Anna and Emily amongst the three long rows of solemn faces greeting us. The opening music repeats six times before the crematorium is full. As I wait by Dad in his wicker casket, my back straightens, I brace myself and feel so far from the boy I used to be.

We make the slow march and Dad weighs heavy on my right shoulder. The entire congregation miss the cue to start singing "Oh Flower of Scotland" so the CD finishes a verse before we do. Luckily, it makes for quite a rousing a cappella rendition. Bev speaks first, shattering the room. Then my godfather, Dad's best friend, raises the ceiling with laughter telling tales of Mike Ziminski and Dad's university love life. When it is my turn, I stand, touching the wicker one last time before ascending the lectern. I speak of cocoons, of sideline red cards and of a father transforming into a brother. Sophie brings things to a close, with a heartbreaking reading of the Scottish poem from Dad and Bev's wedding before hitting play on a favourite number by Canned Heat.

We hold the wake at the Bat and Ball. Despite one person making unintelligent comments about the relationship between mobile phones and brain cancer, I have a good time. Not because I feel relief; no part of me is pleased that Dad is gone. It's more that I'm content with how vivid he feels in my mind. He might not be waiting for us in his cottage armchair – and that knowledge aches so deeply to think about – but this journey has sculpted his presence, made it immortal. In my mind, he is there to answer all my questions. The numerous pints of Guinness help too.

You are my sunshine

Sophie gets nine As and one B in her GCSEs.

Woh, woh, woh, woh

It's 25°C, a Wednesday and my first day back at work. The subterranean studio is exactly as it was but I'm glad to have some projects to occupy my head. Despite being off work since January, these people kept me on full pay and sent me pink lilies when it happened. They never asked for anything and told me I didn't even need to come back. I feel extraordinarily lucky to have found them.

Tonight, Sony have invited Sophie, Bev and me to a memorial in their offices, where Chris Tarrant will be leading the eulogy. It'll be surreal, I'm sure.

Stay stiff, eh

As life begins to normalise, days now pass without significance. That's not to say those days with Dad were always eventful; it's more that I now appreciate just how present I felt. The rawness of these last months isn't something I've ever experienced. Such intense sadness and hopelessness. Living in purgatory, with every high or loving moment tinged with despair. And every low met with a solemn gratitude. But with it, comes colour. I don't think I've ever felt so much, been so sharp and remembered so clearly. It's as if I've shed my base-level emotions for a whole life's worth of feelings. I might have been crushed by an unceasing weight but I've morphed into someone stronger, someone older. I think that's why I was able to say what I needed to say and was able to accept what was to come.

I cannot comprehend the strength of others who are not afforded the luxury of time. Give me the choice between him dying on 13th August the way he did or him vanishing overnight in, say, a car crash on 13th August, I'd choose brain cancer every time. But I know that is inherently selfish. When I think about him, what he endured, the false hope, the goodbyes, the nights alone with his thoughts and his quiet hysteria that arose when reminded that his life was ending, I'm certain he would have taken the crumpled-metal option.

This weaser needs a new biscuit

Emily and I finished today. It's the right decision. We walked for some time on Hampstead Heath before I brought the conversation to a head. She's got too much kindness to call it, but I sense it's mutual.

It's all above me

My single bedroom window looks out onto a pebbledash wall. It is 4.45am and pitch black outside. I spray Dior's Fahrenheit onto a green tartan scarf. Soph and Bev are waiting in the downstairs lobby of Bell Craig Guesthouse, St Andrews. Sophie is carrying Dad.

We walk out of the hotel and down through Murray Park and along the Scores. We can hear the waves beyond the wall. A grassy bank on my left separates us from the residential sea-view properties. After ten minutes the wall ends, and I see the sea. We meander around Bruce Embankment and the ancient golf course. It's 5.15am and we haven't yet seen anyone.

We join West Sands Road, past the 18th's fairway and walk until we reach a small sandy path that leads onto the beach. Flanked by dunes, we reach West Sands beach.

We find the same grassy lip from nine months ago and climb up onto it. Behind us there's a bright-red convertible with its engine running and its roof down. A middle-aged man has chosen the exact same spot and moment to spoil the occasion. Barbs of anger prick as I attempt to shoo him away with my hand. He notices me but doesn't move. My little sister slowly approaches him and within fifteen seconds he's driven away. It reminds me of her kindness and tact.

There, facing the sea, we open the wicker urn. A flick of wind sends bits of him into my mouth and eyes, making me splutter, then laugh. Wiping my face, I watch him fly in a cylindrical motion, a murmuration dancing upon the sands, towards the sea, soaring away from us.

Mrs Craig greets us back at the hotel before 6.00am and asks us what we'd like for breakfast. I order poached eggs, black pudding and twelve sachets of ketchup.

I want some cake and a cigar

California. Dad's rented a convertible pink Jeep, and to Mum's consternation, has taught me the lyrics to Canned Heat's "Going Up the Country". I'm nearly six, sat in the back, and singing them as loudly as I can.

I'm going, I'm going
Where the water tastes like wine
I'm going where the water tastes like wine
We can jump in the water
Stay drunk all the time.

A note from the author

Dearest Sophie,

I know you said you'll never read this book, so these are likely to be destination-less words. But if you ever do, I hope I haven't hurt you. I hope it hasn't warped your own memories of that time. I hope I've managed to capture a man who meant so much to us, in a way that makes you smile.
I love you.

Your brother,
Freddy.

Acknowledgements

On 29 July 2011, Bev rushed out Pond Cottage's door grabbing the only notebook in sight. It was a luminous blue, ring-bound *Finding Nemo* one. I've had it with me ever since I started writing this. Without that book and her notes, the precise chronology and detail of this book would not have been possible. Thank you for keeping it, for lending it and for the pillar of strength you became. Thank you to the surgeons of Seven Hills Mumbai and St George's – without you we would have lost him far sooner. To the doctors and nurses of the Royal Marsden, thank you for getting us as much time as we could have with him. Thank you to the angels of Phyllis Tuckwell and Macmillan. And to Sarah, the nurse who lived with us, stayed up with us, spoke with us and helped us all, thank you.

I once described the book I was attempting to write to a new friend on a train to Oxford. That friend, Evie Dunne, became my editor and agent. She believed in it. She's read it more times than anyone and her guidance and persistence are the reason you're here, reading these words.

Between drafts one and two of this book something changed; that change was the result of the help of Katrin MacGibbon. Thank you for your brilliance. To Rebecca

Nicolson, Aurea Carpenter and everyone at Short Books, thank you for believing in something so precious to me. Anna Ginsburg, thank you for lighting me up, picking up your phone, taking me out and staying the night. To Iona McLaren, thank you for being the first to endorse this, having your backing carried *Toast* forward and upwards. To Jon Gray for designing the wonderful cover. To Philly Malicka, thank you for lending me your words. And thank you to my friends Olivia Ovenden, Oliver Pym, Harriet Lowson, Martin Plimmer, Jane Finigan, Philippa Beaumont, Paddy Treacy, Oliver Leonard Wit, Bertie Troughton, Harriet Moore, Oscar Laughridge, George Butler, Sonia Delesalle-Stolper, Ed Cumming and Lara Prendergast for lending your time and for all the little and large things you did.

The last words of this book belong to Constance Booth. She's nurtured it at every stage and helped me more than she would ever give herself credit for. Writing can be a solo venture but from the very beginning I've felt like she's been running alongside me. Thank you, MC.